THE TRIUMPHS OF FAITH

THE TRIUMPHS OF FAITH

BY

G. CAMPBELL MORGAN, D.D.

Author of
"The Crises of the Christ," "Searchlights from the Word," etc.

LONDON:
PICKERING & INGLIS LTD.

Pickering & Inglis Ltd.

33 New Bridge Street, London, E.C.4
229 Bothwell Street, Glasgow, C.2
59 Cross Street, Manchester, 2
56 Grainger Street, Newcastle upon Tyne
5 Hope Way, Liverpool, 8
29 George IV Bridge, Edinburgh, 1
Loizeaux Bros., 19 West 21st Street, New York
Home Evangel, 418 Church Street, Toronto, 2

BOOK
PRODUCTION
WAR ECONOMY
STANDARD

Made and Printed in Great Britain   810436

Preface

THE answer of God to a perplexed prophet (Habakkuk) was the revelation of the basic principle of human life: "The just shall live by faith." That statement is repeated three times in the New Testament; from the pen of Paul in Romans and Galatians, and by the writer of the letter to the Hebrews.

The Roman letter is the document of human salvation. Galatians is the document of liberty rightly interpreted. Hebrews is pre-eminently the document of faith.

John declares, "This is the victory that hath overcome the world, even our faith."

The writer of the letter to the Hebrews illustrates this principle in a great paragraph (x. 37—xii. 3). He gathers his illustrations from the history of the Hebrew people. This book consists of lectures in consideration of that whole paragraph. It goes back, however, and starts with the human race, in the elders—Abel, Enoch, Noah. Then, beginning with Abraham, it passes over the history of the Hebrew people, showing in varied ways how their triumph in every way was always the result of faith.

Contents

I

"My Righteous One shall Live by Faith"

SCRIPTURE LESSON - - Habakkuk ii. 1-5; Romans i. 16, 17;
Galatians iii. 10, 11; Hebrews x. 36-39

"My righteous One shall live by faith" - Hebrews x. 38 (R.V.)

T HE subject of faith has occupied my mind very much in
these strange and perplexing days through which we have been
passing. The word is the commonplace of our holy religion.
The word, however, is oftentimes vitiated by false or partial
interpretation. With this in my mind I have been driven back to
the great classic passage in the Bible which covers the whole area
of human life, this eleventh chapter of the epistle to the Hebrews.

Neither the prelude to chapter xi (x. 37-39) nor the text I have
taken therefrom defines or illustrates faith. In this prelude we
have the declaration of a principle, and a revelation of a philosophy
of life. In that way we approach them now. The words were
cited by the writer, from Habakkuk. They also occur in two
other places in the New Testament. The three passages we read,
one in Romans, one in Galatians, and here in this tenth chapter of
Hebrews. The declaration of it in the Old Testament, and the
citations of it in the New, are very significant.

Let us first of all consider the setting of the words in the Old
Testament, and their citations in the New; then attempt to consider
the principle of a philosophy of life revealed in these words.

The setting of the text in Habakkuk is most suggestive. This
prophecy may be described as an account of the agnosticism of
faith. It is not so much a prophecy as a story of the experience of
one man. That man was a prophet unquestionably, and in that
sense it is a prophecy through an experience, which he has recorded
for us in this brief book that bears his name.

These were dark days in the history of the people of God.
The national conditions were appalling. Concerning that fact
he first spoke in the presence of God. He spoke of the prevalence
of violence, and iniquity, and pride abounding in the national
life. The international situation was threatening. Enemies

seemed to be closing in upon this nation, and the difficulty for Habakkuk was this, that God seemed to be negative, waiting. He seemed to be doing nothing. That is how the prophecy opened.

Then we are told that God answered him. Again reverently to change the wording, in an expression of the truth; God said to him in effect: It is true you think I am doing nothing, but I am. I am at work; but, if I told you what I am doing, you would not believe it. Then God did tell him what He was doing, that He was raising up the most cruel and brutish people of the times, the Chaldeans, to be His instrument for the carrying out of His purpose in the world, and among His people.

Habakkuk then said in effect: This is worse than ever. It seemed bad enough if God were doing nothing; but now He tells me that He is using these people, the terror of the nation, for His own purpose. I do not understand it. I will get me to the watch-tower, and I will wait. In that moment Habakkuk came to the greatest decision that was possible for a human soul in those circumstances. The man of faith has often been perplexed, overwhelmed with the difficulties of the situation, and the hour in which he lives; and more troubled about this than anything else, that God seems to be doing nothing!

We have often heard that in recent times. What is God doing? Why doesn't God do something? God is still saying the same amazing thing: I am at work, though if I told you, you would not believe, or understand, but the fact remains. I am raising up and using in the working out of My purposes in the world, the very people or peoples concerning whom you are filled with dread. When God says that, it is time for us to shut our mouths. That is what Habakkuk did. But he did not shut his ears. Again in effect, he said: Well, I am not questioning what God has said, but I do not understand it. I will get me to the watch-tower, and I will wait for God.

The trouble with us is that too often we do not wait to see what God would say to us. In these circumstances of helplessness the prophet decided to wait for God, and having so decided, God answered him. Mark his words: "And the Lord answered me." What did He say? He sent him a vision. This does not mean He actually appeared to him at all. The Hebrew word for vision means very simply a mental conception, an outlook, a revelation. The oracle of God spoke to him: Let me give you a vision, an interpretation, a final point from which to view all the circumstances, and events; and then write it on tablets, not that he who reads may run, but he who runs may read. This man who is busily occupied in a thousand ways—running, tearing along—make it so plain that as he passes by, he can see it. That is the claim, that the vision should be written on tablets, made plain, so conspicuously that the running, racing man may see it. Do not be in a hurry. Tarry for it, wait for it. It will surely come. That is the simple, initial statement.

What was the vision? As we go back to Habakkuk we find that after that charge, that declaration of a vision, and a charge to write it and make it plain, the vision is declared, "Behold, his soul is puffed up, it is not upright in him; but the just shall live by his faith." That is all. The remainder of the chapter is an almost detailed exposition of the first half of the vision, "Behold, his soul is puffed up." There is no exposition of the second half. It does not need it. It is a simple statement.

We have here two philosophies of life; first, that of the puffed-up. I like the translation, but let me slightly alter it, "the swollen." It is a graphic figure of pride and self-sufficiency. That is one philosophy of life, puffed up, swollen, filled with pride, filled with self-sufficiency. The other figure is this, "the righteous one shall live by faith"; a sense of certainty in spite of appearances, and a condition of consequent trustworthiness; for the word "faith" here is rendered by some "faithfulness." The meaning of the Hebrew word, as also the Greek, has the two-fold application. When Jesus said to Thomas, "Be not faithless, but believing," He did not merely say, You should have faith, but, having faith you should be trustworthy. It is the same thought here.

So the whole meaning is covered in one of the simplest of sentences. I use it resolutely and reverently, in some senses the mightiest sentence in the Book of God. It is the revelation of the true philosophy of the Biblical history from the primeval movement in Genesis to the Apocalyptic Revelation. The theme all circles round this, "The just shall live by faith," The two issues and the two philosophies are there.

Read the rest of the second chapter of Habakkuk for the picture of the puffed-up, and make any application of it to the age in which we are living. John Wesley said he read the newspaper to see how God is governing the world. When I am tired of the newspaper I go back to the Book. When I am tired of the trivialities and the prattle and the toys of time, I go back to the voices of the old Hebrew prophets, and place the measuring line of Habakkuk's philosophy on the disturbances everywhere in the world at the present hour. Yes, let us wait! Read this chapter through at your leisure, honestly, and think as you read; and you will see that the ultimate issue of the swelled-up, or swollen attitude to life is explosion. Watch the balloon that the child is playing with. Look at it, blow it up, and keep on blowing it. If you do, Puff! It is gone! By the swelling it bursts. That is the story of human history, and it is the story of individual life as well. The soul that is self-centred and self-sufficient, the soul that is arrogant, and struts in the presence of Almighty God, sooner or later collapses, and there is break-up. The balloon is pricked and bursts.

What about the other? There is no chapter about the other. One word only is needed. What is it? "The just shall *live.*" The word marks power of continuity. The word marks reality, the realisation of victory and life. "Live by faith"! How? By being not proud, self-centred, self-satisfied. The swollen ends in dissolution. Faith ends in a perfect realisation. That is the setting of the text.

The citations of this statement in the New Testament are remarkable in their placing, in Romans, Galatians, and Hebrews.

The letter to the Romans is pre-eminently the document of human salvation. Galatians is pre-eminently the document of liberty rightly interpreted. Hebrews, from first to last, is pre-eminently the document of faith. In these three great writings dealing with salvation, liberty, and faith, these words are cited, and in remarkable connections.

The apostle, writing to the Romans, said, "I am not ashamed of the Gospel." The Gospel is the good news that tells how men can realise all that in which they have failed. There it is, instantly flashing like a central, burning light on the page; "The just shall live by faith." That is the issue of the Gospel.

The Galatian letter is the document of freedom, that deals with the emancipation from every yoke of bondage that can be placed upon the human soul. "It breaks the power of cancelled sin." It breaks the tyranny of the law, of every imprisoning habit. In the midst of it Paul says, "The just shall live by faith." He shall enter into freedom, find salvation in the Gospel, enter the joy of absolute freedom, and the principle is faith.

So lastly, the letter to the Hebrews is pre-eminently the document of faith, and reveals the principle of triumph over all sorts of conditions as revealed in the eleventh chapter. But in every case it is the Gospel for the world. Faith is the principle of life. It is the emancipation from all tyranny. Faith is the principle of liberty. It is the secret of victory in all circumstances.

It remains only for us to consider the principle as declared. That principle is revealed in this contrast between pride and self-sufficiency on the one hand, and faith or confidence on the other hand. Pride and self-sufficiency are equal to provocative exploits. Let us make no mistake about that. Not only as we glance back over the Biblical history, but look out on the world as it is. Pride and self-sufficiency are equal to great exploits. But look back and see the lust of self-sufficiency, and all exploits growing out of it will sooner or later collapse. Whether it be a man or a nation, the same thing is true.

On the other hand, confidence is equal to many things, to exploits oftentimes mysterious, and far more wonderful than the exploits of the proud. Look again at the eleventh chapter of Hebrews, and see there what faith is equal to, and in every case it ends in vindication of itself.

Two philosophies of life. Not only the contrasts are true, but the positive declaration. Faith is the principle of life. Not decay, not death, not dissolution; but the principle that furnishes, that continues, that achieves.

But let it at once be said that this message is very unfinished, I will not say inadequate. Faith is not defined in our text. A definition is found in the eleventh chapter, and the assertion is merely what the writer of this letter cited from Habakkuk. It is an assertion, sharp, clear, challenging, bold, daring; but no illustrations are given in the text. They are all massed in the eleventh chapter. Yet we do not stay there. That eleventh chapter is unfinished, just as in some ways the Acts of the Apostles is unfinished. We might go on multiplying illustrations a thousand, a million-fold.

Faith must be interpreted by this Biblical literature. Faith may be a creed, valuable in its way, yet having no living power. Faith may represent something far short of the Biblical meaning. But Faith in the Bible is always something that reaches through until it touches God; through the smoke of battle, through the murk and misery that appal us, through the darkness of the hour, through the threatening forces of evil that seem so rampant—through, and beyond that, behind that, nay above that, to God. Faith is that which reaches Him and touches Him.

The attestation of the truth of the great declaration, of its two-fold nature, is attested in human history of the world. We remember the story of Alexander, that when he had conquered the whole known world he went to see the philosopher, Diogenes, living in his tub. Alexander stood at the entrance and called to him. A voice said, "Who art thou?" He said, "I am Alexander, the master of the world." "Is that so? Get out of my sunlight." The great philosopher was able to dismiss as an arrogant fool the master of the world. Diogenes added, "Go, and learn to be wise. Conquer thine own spirit, and take no light thou canst not give." The proud and the puffed-up, and the great explosion!

Augustus Cæsar came nearer to hegemony, or governing the whole world, than even Alexander. How did it end? This applied to pagan rule:

"Rome has perished! Write that word
In the blood that she has spilt;
Perished hopeless and abhorred,
Deep in ruin, as in guilt."

That is what happened.

So at this hour, or near to our own time. What about Napoleon? We could name other names also. No despot who is governing as the result of pride and self-sufficiency can possibly continue. There must inevitably be an explosion, a dissolution. If we are living by faith, then though it may be through scourgings and mockings and perils and dangers, we shall arrive, for "the just shall live by faith."

II

The Nature of Faith

SCRIPTURE LESSON - - - - - 2 Kings vi. 13-17
"Now faith is the assurance of things hoped for, the proving of
things not seen" - - - - - Hebrews xi. 1

THESE words constitute a declaration of the nature of faith.
Faith is really the subject of the whole letter; for its purpose unquestionably was to stablish and strengthen the early Hebrew
Christians, who felt that they had lost so much as they had turned
from the splendid ritual and ceremony of the Hebrew faith to the
simpler things that are in Christ Jesus. This letter was written to
save them from that form of lack of faith which becomes apostasy.

The history of this world's progress is that of the triumph of
faith. Faith is a paradox, something contrary to reason, and yet
true. In my boyhood I loved horses. I still love them. The law
of the road is a paradox, and I was taught in rhyme:

> "The law of the road is a paradox quite,
>   And that you may tell by my song,
> If you go to the left, you are sure to go right;
>   And if you go right, you go wrong!"

That is a perfect paradox; apparently wrong, contrary to reason,
and yet true. So faith is always a paradox. Faith sings in prison,
and not when it gets out of prison. Oh, it may sing when it gets
out, but it antedates its escape by singing in prison, as witness Paul
and Silas. Faith fights in chains. Paul said, "Remember my
bonds." Faith works and accomplishes things without any of the
tools upon which men seem so largely to depend.

It might be good to make a list of the literature of the prison,
that which reveals faith triumphant. Jeremiah, Ezekiel, or Paul,
and John. All in prison. Or down the centuries, 200 years ago,
John Bunyan, whose great drama was composed in prison. The
prophecies of Jeremiah and Ezekiel, the writings of Paul and John,
the matchless beauty of Bunyan, were all created by faith. If the
test of a word is a work, if the test of a creed is a creation, if the test

15

of a root is a fruit, faith is abundantly vindicated through all the
running centuries.

We ask this question then: Why is it that faith thus triumphs?
This wonderful section of the letter, as we have seen, really commences in the previous chapter (x). There the writer quotes from
Habakkuk when he declares the great principles of the victorious
life, "The just shall live by faith." We ask then: What is this faith?
In this study we commence to answer that question. In the said
words we have a clear-cut crystallized definition of faith. The
first word of the text is "Now," the little word that links the
argument of the letter directly with what the writer said pre-
viously, "My righteous one shall live by faith." Missing out the
intervening words for the moment, he said, "Now." Faith is the
assurance of things hoped for, the proving of things not seen.

Before proceeding, I want to say two things of a general nature.
This is the only definition of faith to be found in the Bible. There
are explanations and applications, but here is a clear-cut definition,
and the only one. Again, the definition is not complete. This is a
definition of faith in the abstract. There is a concrete fact, consideration of which we do not reach here, but to which we come
in our subsequent studies.

There are in these words two very simple and self-evident
things. This definition first of all reveals the spheres in which
faith operates; and within the definition, that which so operates
in those spheres.

First then, the sphere of operation. "Faith is the assurance of
things hoped for, the proving of *things not seen*." The two spheres,
nevertheless one in the last analysis, "things hoped for, things not
seen." Those are the two realms in which faith becomes operative.
There is no need to illustrate that, apart from the Biblical literature,
although it could be done. It is true in every realm of life.

"Things hoped for." What are they? Things not yet attained,
things not in our possession. "Who hopeth for that which he
seeth?" We enter the realm of the future when we speak of
things hoped for. Let us ask ourselves: For what are we hoping?
I am not thinking on the level of the dust now, where

> "The earth of a dusty to-day,
> Is the dust of an earthy to-morrow."

I am thinking on high levels now. What are we hoping for?
The realisation of our ideals, the ultimate victory of good, compensation for all the things which have to be endured, and the

enduring of which is contributing towards that ultimate compensation. We hope for a time when in human life and affairs an even balance shall be struck. Take any position you will. Call it what our thinkers call it sometimes, "the golden age," or think of it in terms of the poet, who sang of

> "The far-off Divine event,
> To which the whole creation moves."

"Things hoped for." There may be times when hope seems to flicker to the lowest, and hardly gives any light. We have all known such times; but, the things hoped for, the aspirations of the soul, that is the sphere in which faith operates.

The second phrase, "things not seen." That is difficult. At least it seems to be so. It does seem easy, naturally, to believe in things we can see. Faith does not operate there at all. We do not need any faith to believe in things seen. We have all heard the old saying, "Seeing is believing." Is that true? No! Believing is being sure without seeing. Faith operates there in the presence of things that eye has not seen, things that have not entered into the understanding of the mind. That is the realm of faith.

Are there any such things? There is only one answer to that. As we read the wonderful illustrations of faith given us by this writer, he says of one man, that "he endured, as seeing Him Who is invisible." A great and glorious statement! Such an absurd thing, is it not, you worldly-wise man? Seeing the invisible! That is faith. That is the sphere in which faith operates in the spiritual world in the midst of which we are always living, even in the dust of the city. The unseen things, the hidden forces that are everywhere, if we could see them. We cry out, "Master, what shall we do?" But the man who can see, says, "Lord, open his eyes," and the Lord in the ancient story opened his eyes, those eyes that are more than human sight, and "Behold, the mountain was full of horses and chariots of fire round about." The young man had not seen them, but they were there, unseen things. What a wonderful story that is, and how perfectly it illustrates this; the faith of Elisha, and the sight that came to his servant. Some of us may be thinking of those lines of Wesley, in his great hymn:

> "Lo, to faith's enlightened sight,
> All the mountain flamed with light.
> Hell is nigh, but God is nigher,
> Circling us with hosts of fire."

2

We cannot see these things, but they are there, and faith enters into that realm.

With great reverence, Jesus had this vision when His hour of travail came. "Thinkest thou that I cannot beseech My Father, and He shall even now send Me more than twelve legions of angels?" He did not ask for them, but He saw them, and saw the possibility. Faith entered into the realm of the unseen. When we cease to believe in unseen things, hope dies, and the song is silent, and fighting ends, and the work is abandoned. To quote again words concerning Moses, he "endured as seeing Him Who is invisible."

The "things hoped for" is the sphere in which faith operates; the realm into which we climb when thought becomes longing, aspiration, and strong desire. Faith enters into that realm.

Secondly, "the things unseen," the things that cannot be proven mathematically. There are so many things we cannot prove mathematically that we know are so. No one can prove that the woman he or she called mother, was their mother. Produce the birth certificate. That is worthless. But we know; faith has entered into the realm of mystery, and we are sure. That is the sphere of operations.

Let us turn now to the definition, which is abstract, and not final. What is faith? It is "assurance, proving." Those are the two words of the Revised Version. The Authorised Version reads: "Faith is the substance of things hoped for, the evidence of things not seen." The Revisers have substituted "assurance" for "substance," and "proving" instead of "evidence."

But the Revised Version still lacks something meant by the writer. A far better rendering of that word, *hupostasis*, is the simple word confidence; "faith is the confidence of things hoped for." Confidence! Certainty which produces action. It is not merely confidence in the sense of being sure that it is so; but a confidence that becomes conviction. That is faith exactly, confidence, certainty of things hoped for; certainty of the ultimate realisation of our ideals, the ultimate victory of good, and the striking presently of an even balance everywhere, with a great sense of compensation and realisation. Faith is sure about things hoped for.

What is "proving"? What is "evidence"? Evidence is proving offered. We give evidence, which means we are offering proof. The Revisers have improved the old rendering, by translating "proving." There is an added shade of meaning here.

If evidence is proof offered, proving is proof offered and accepted. It is not merely that evidence is given, but it is so given that it produces actual conviction. "Faith is the confidence of things hoped for, the conviction of things not seen." The writer here is proceeding from effect to cause. What is the effect? Confidence of things hoped for. What is the cause? Conviction of things not seen.

Here is the mental process. Faith, first, is a conviction of the reality of the unseen. Secondly, confidence that all the terms will be fulfilled, that the vision will be translated into victory. Faith enters that realm. Conviction of things not seen is the confidence in things hoped for. The conviction of the builder is the confidence that the city will be built. The conviction concerning the unseen realities is the confidence of the realisation of ideals. It is an abstract definition, but what a definition! How it gives us pause for thought!

Can we apply it individually, and to the Christian Church, and to the world at large? Unless faith enters that realm of unseen things, and becomes conviction, there is no certainty about faith at all, there is no guarantee. It is faith that grasps the reality, reaches out to the unseen, and then focuses upon it, acts upon it; and that hope is no longer mere hope, in a speculative sense, but becomes a great certainty.

These are the things that have created all the great victories and triumphs of our human progress, so far as there has been progress. Men first become sure of the unseen, and when sure of the unseen they become sure of the ultimate victory of the ideal. If we are not sure of the unseen, we are without hope, because without God in the world. In the presence of such a definition I take the language of the man who came once to Jesus and said, "Lord, I believe, help Thou mine unbelief."

III

Fundamentals in the Exercise of Faith

SCRIPTURE LESSON -   -   -   - Mark xi. 12-14 and 20-25

"He that cometh to God must believe that He is, and that He is a
Rewarder of them that seek after Him"   -   Hebrews xi. 6

IN our last study we were considering a definition of faith in
the abstract. Faith is "confidence in things hoped for, the conviction
of things not seen." However in neither the words cited in
Habakkuk nor in that definition contained in the first verse of this
chapter have we struck the deepest note. Faith is there seen to be
an activity in two realms, those of things hoped for, and the unseen
things. We do not see that upon which faith builds.

In the words of the text we come to bedrock, as it declares
the fundamental facts of the activity of faith in that duplicate sense.
I say a duplicate sense, because faith may have a hundred and one
suggestions; and may make many suggestions to the mind when
reading the illustrations of faith in the Bible. This word, however,
brings us face to face with something fundamental. "He that
cometh to God must believe that He is, and that He is a Rewarder
of them that seek after Him."

The Bible assumes these two things. From the first it assumes
that God is. It assumes, moreover, that He is the Rewarder of
those that seek Him. The Bible never argues for either of these
things, nor did the great men of the Bible, presented to us in their
messages to men. With profound reverence I may say that Jesus
Himself never argued for the existence of God, nor concerning His
availability to men. He assumed them. He took them for
granted. He proceeded in His teaching, and in His mighty work
upon these very assumptions. There may be arguments about the
love of God, the justice of God, the care of God, but never about
His existence, and this simple fact that God and man may have
dealings with each other; that God is available to human life.
Indeed, the old singer dismisses with contempt the man who
doubts that. He says the man who does not believe in God is a
fool. Faith bursts into the realm of things hoped for, of things
not seen; and faith becomes confident, and enters into covenant.

We will stay first with the central idea expressed by this writer when he says, "He that cometh to God"; and then look at the declared conditions.

We must believe that God is, and that He is a Rewarder. "He that cometh to God." For a long time, in my reading of this passage I thought of it as referring to prayer. While I have by no means given up that idea, I have come to see that it means far more than that. Prayer is involved, but there is more than prayer in coming to God. Simply and inclusively, the writer means by coming to God, approaching God, drawing near to God, getting into direct and living and vital contact with God. "He that cometh to God." Coming to God is having communication with Him.

Now we realise that a man can believe in God in certain ways, and yet never get into communication with Him. A man may have a perfectly orthodox creed. But a very orthodox thinking about God may be infinitely removed from contact with God; and it is contact with God that is rewarded here. That is what faith is for. Faith is not merely acceptance of certain truths about God. Faith goes through the truths to God Himself. "He that cometh to God." Simply and inclusively that means to approach God, to get near to God, to put oneself into communication with Him.

That approach to God has two main ideas. The simplest of all is that to come to God is to speak to God. To come to God is to hear God speak to us. We must not divorce these two ideas. That, of course, is prayer. This word does refer to prayer, but to far more. It refers to a man talking to God. There are two functions of the human soul in the matter of speech to God. The first is prayer, the second is praise. I put them in that order because I think in human experience, prayer always precedes praise. In living experience we begin to pray before we begin to praise, which is the truest and highest function of speech. Prayer is the first experience, and praise is the highest and the last.

That, of course, is the whole subject of worship. We come to the Table of the Lord. We do not come there to pray but to praise. I love the word which describes the Table as the Eucharist. What is that? Simply the offering of praise, or worship. We make a great mistake if we come to the Table to confess sins. That should have been done before we came. If we have not sought for cleansing before we come, we have no place at the Table. Therefore here supremely we approach God, speaking to Him in praise.

But to come near to God means not only that we come to speak to Him, but we come to be quiet, to listen. In that call to quietness there are two things: silence and reception. There can be no reception of the speech of God directly to the soul of man until man is quiet. Do we take time to listen? It is an old and familiar thing to say. People say, God does not speak to men as He did in the great records of the past. God does not speak to men to-day as He did to Abraham and to Moses. Might it not be far truer to put that in another form? Men do not listen as Abraham did. Man is not waiting to hear what God has to say as Moses did. Approach to God means time to be quiet. When the last prayer is uttered, when the last note of praise is silent; then in the silence, the heart can wait and listen to Him. I have never done that without having heard Him speak. Not necessarily with an articulate voice; but so surely as I have heard, and stopped my hurry, and bustle, and rushing, and turmoil, and ceased giving attention to the babel of voices and sounds beating all around me; and have said, "Lord, speak to me," He has done so, often in rebuke, and constantly in love. But He speaks.

Now he who comes to God, who approaches God, he who makes communication with God, which means freedom of utterance in His presence; and in the silence listens to what He would say, what are the conditions of that coming? They are so simply, clearly, and succinctly stated here that we need not stay with them. We will but emphasize the things we know. "He that cometh to God must believe that He is, and that He is a Rewarder of those that seek after Him." It is a simple statement, but it is a sublime conception. The inclusive condition is that of faith, confidence, and conviction with regard to His Being; and with regard to His attitude toward certain human disability.

If we come to God we must believe that He is. Can one really come to God if we do not believe that He is? A man may say No, and perhaps that is why we do not come to Him, and do not make contact with Him. It is not easy to believe that He is. How often that is affirmed. I am of the contrary opinion. I declare that it is the easiest thing in human life to believe in God. Effort is not required. Effort is required to disbelieve, rather than to believe.

Read again the story of Helen Keller—that marvellous and matchless story which reflects such glory upon Miss Sullivan, the woman who cared for her and taught her, a child silent, deaf, dumb, and blind, and yet reached her. When she had led Helen Keller a certain distance, she sought someone to talk to her about God. The man she approached was Bishop Phillips Brooks. He came to see her, and when he tried to bring to her the idea of God as existing, suddenly Helen Keller's face became radiant as she said to him, "I see what you mean, but I have known that all the time." All through the years she had known God, and that God is. So simple, so tender. Can you find me a little child who does not believe in God, save where that child has been brought up in utter ignorance? It is the natural instinct of a child to believe in God. All simple souls believe in God. It is a universal conviction. There may be differing views about God, but are there any who have no conception of God? That is the first necessity. If lines of proof are asked for, I shall appeal to imagination, to reason, and then to historic manifestation.

I appeal first to the imagination. There was a book published many years ago, Paley's "Natural Theology," one of the greatest books ever published. In it he argued from design that God was evidenced everywhere. Grasping a handful of sand, and looking at it, no one would be able to count the grains, for there are so many. Again, take a watch and hold it in your hand, whether you stop to argue concerning its natural movement, your mind would run ahead to the fact that somewhere there is a watchmaker. That is a very clear illustration of what Paley meant by evidence from design. We cannot imagine a watch without a watchmaker. Apply that to the universe in which we live. If that watch argues a watchmaker, what does this universe argue? Even if I am told watches have improved since Paley's time, that does not for a moment invalidate the argument, but rather enhances it. The better watch proves a more skilful watchmaker, but the watchmaker is there. It is a fact that the mechanism of the universe has been proved far more complex than our fathers believed; but are the growing proofs of the complexity of the universe any less an attestation of the mind of a Creator? It is easy to believe in God.

Think for a moment of the creation. Creation without intelligence? Order without arrangement? Order is everywhere. Put it to the test. Go into an apple orchard, and gather the fruit, and you will find that the leaves on the twig grow in spirals, and the sixth is always exactly over the first. Did that just happen— happen a myriad times? No, there is method behind it: Somebody Who knows. Go at harvest-time, and take an ear of corn in the field; and you will not find a single ear with an odd number of rows. Somebody counts! A man tells me that all is without God. I do not, and cannot believe that. I must believe that He is. That is the appeal to the imagination.

Then there is an appeal to reason. That has been involved in what I have said. Can we imagine man without God? Some people seem to. Surely they must be shockingly ashamed of their ancestry. If a man as he is to-day—I care not whether good or bad—surely there is some mind behind this creation, surely some intelligence that accounts for such a being. In appealing to reason, all I want to say is this. It is far easier for me to believe that He is, than that He is not. I must believe that. I must start there.

And yet we are not left to such illustrations. Light is beating all around us concerning God. It broke in upon human intelligence nineteen hundred years ago, when God was manifested in the flesh. The Man of Nazareth made His claim to be one with God. He exhorted men to believe in God; and His victories were always those of leading men to that conviction, and to that understanding. If we would approach Him, we must begin there, and believe that God is.

But we may believe all that, and yet fail to make contact with God. That is why the second statement of condition is of vital importance. We must also believe that He is the Rewarder of them that seek after Him. That is not belief in the moral government of God, though that, of course, is necessarily involved. It is a belief that He does not and cannot abandon man, created in His own image and in His own likeness. A man may say that he believes in God, and in His omnipotence, and yet say that He is careless of man. It is impossible to make me believe that. Whether it be the result of scientific investigation or the result of the Biblical declaration, man is the crowning glory of creation as we know it in this world. I am only an individual in this world, and there are worlds that I have not yet seen. My thought of heaven is not merely one place, but a universe. What exercises we shall have when we investigate God's great universe! But in this earth, the highest work and form of being is man; and the highest thing in man is his moral character, his sentiment or conviction. God must have to do with that man, and He must have to do with that man morally, if He is a Rewarder. Then He must be available to man.

We must be careful here, because there are men who do not reach God, and men that God does not reach. In a certain way He reaches all men, for in Him we live and move and have our being. But there are men who are not conscious of Him, they have no dealings with Him, He cannot have dealings with them. He cannot reach them. He cannot tell them His secrets. "The

secret of the Lord is with them that fear Him." He can com-
municate with such. So He is the Rewarder of them that seek
after Him. It is a great word, those who diligently seek Him.
It conveys effort in its simplicity and sublimity.

One can walk through the cornfields, and across the meadows
by the river bank, and over the mountains, and never touch Him.
We must "seek Him." The word has all the force of investigation,
of demand made upon us. Why should I use any other words than
those that Jesus uttered, "Ask . . . seek . . . knock"? They describe
the attitude of the soul to which God can make His response. He
is the Rewarder of those that seek after Him. These are the people
who "ask, seek, knock," who reach God, and whom He can reach.

But is that possible? The first proof that it is possible is found
in the ability of man to do this very thing. God has so created
man that he can ask, he can seek, and he can knock. There are no
half measures in Nature, we are told. If God gives a fish fins, there
is water in which to use them. If God gives a bird wings, there is
air in which it can fly. If God gives to man the capacity to seek
Him, there is the possibility of an answer to his seeking. We may
therefore conclude that God is a Rewarder, which is testified by the
experience of man. If testimony is to be accepted as evidence on
any subject, it must be accepted here. Multitudes of people have
testified to the fact in their lives that having sought, they have
found; having asked, they have been answered; having knocked
at the door, it was swung open, and God has come to them.

The final proof is the testimony of the Man of Nazareth, Who,
whatever doubts we may have concerning some of the things He
said, as to what they meant, has left no room for doubts that He
believed, and intended men to believe that God is available to souls,
will answer them, will reward them, will come to them in grace,
in succour, in strength, in love, in help—when they seek after Him.

Let us consider, in conclusion, the teaching involved. In the
whole of the Biblical revelation, from beginning to end, belief in
God is manifest as in One Who knows, and Whose wisdom is
infinite. There is no journey to take to find Him. He is all-
powerful. He is alive. How easy it is to come to Him, for
perfect love casts out fear.

> "This is the God we adore,
>   Our faithful infallible Friend;
>   His love is as great as His power,
>   And knows neither measure nor end."

If we believe He is a Rewarder, it means we believe He is interested in us, an infinite mystery and wonder, something that baffles the intellect. Amid all the wonders of the far-flung splendours of the universe, here am I, insignificant, a grain of dust, and yet God is interested in me! I think it is well to advise young people to go back and study the Old Testament, and particularly the book which some people consider dry and uninteresting—Leviticus. There we see how interested God is in man, in the very simplest matters. He is interested in what we wear, according to the climate, and the texture of wool or cotton. The clothing ordered then was hygienic and necessary in that climate, for the people. That is illustrated all through the Bible. "Thou shalt not seethe a kid in its mother's milk." Have we ever stopped to think about that command? I see His interest in man, in him, and his home, his furniture, his reading, in everything. He is a Rewarder.

That means His purpose is a purpose of blessing; and He will bestow it for ever upon people that will seek after Him. How easy it is. No persuasion is necessary. "Nothing in my hand I bring." I may rest assured that there will be no refusal, except the refusal of infinite Love, and His "No" is as much a proof of His love, and often more so than if He gave the thing asked for. He never denies save in love. "No good thing will He withhold from them that walk uprightly."

Yet I would remind you that the text marks the note of urgency. Belief means more than conviction; it means obedience. It means trusting, and venturing upon God, coming to Him, speaking to Him, listening to Him, daring everything upon His word. That is the condition to which God can appeal. He who comes to God, comes to One Who rewards that kind of coming.

We should not forget the setting of the text. The section begins in the tenth chapter. Let us go further back, to the beginning of the letter. There we find that God, Who spoke to the fathers by divers portions and in divers manners, has spoken in His Son; and He stands to us in the place of God, for He is God. Faith in Christ is faith in God; and he that comes, must believe that He is. So humanity is brought face to face with the Person of Christ. As we believe in Him, faith is passing through the manifestation to the thing manifested, and we are finding God; and that is the bedrock of faith.

IV

Faith and History: as to Nature and Interpretation

SCRIPTURE LESSON - - - Psalm xix
"Therein the elders had witness borne to them.
By faith we understand that the worlds have been framed by
the word of God, so that what is seen hath not been made out of
things which do appear" - - - Hebrew xi. 2, 3

BY citation from Habakkuk, the writer of this letter has declared faith to be the true philosophy of life: "My righteous one shall live by faith." He has, moreover, defined faith in the abstract. "Faith is the assurance of things hoped for, the proving of things not seen." In the rest of this chapter (xi) we have abounding illustrations of the power and the victory of faith. The writer has selected his illustrations from the stream of history, from Abel to Jesus. The consummation is reached, not in the eleventh, but the twelfth chapter.

In the words of our text, before dealing with personalities, he shows faith in its relation to human history as a whole. I know of no passage which has suffered more from misunderstanding, due to faulty translation. Let us, therefore, follow three lines of consideration, first attempting a careful examination of the passage itself; then observing the statement of its double declaration. So we shall find its interpretation of history.

I have dogmatically said that this passage has been misunderstood largely through faulty translation. Notice first of all that the writer says, "Therein the elders had witness borne to them." The Old Version read, "Through faith the elders obtained a good report." Some may say those two translations mean the same thing. They may, but they may be very different. The Authorised Version suggests a record concerning the elders. When we went to school, we took home at the end of the year a good report—at least some did—but it was a report! That is how we have understood this, the elders had a good report. Their marks were good. But if we take the translation, "the elders had witness borne to them," not about them, but to them, the form suggests a record

27

the elders gained, and received; a good report, they had witness borne to them. They were not talking. They were listening. They were not reading something said *about* them. They were listening to something said *to* them. "Through faith the elders had witness borne to them." I do not object to the Old rendering, provided we understand the meaning of the word "obtained."

Then again. "By faith we understand that the worlds have been framed by the word of God." That is constantly understood as a reference to the material universe, to creation, a reference to the great phrase, "In the beginning God created the heavens and the earth." That is a glaring error. The word used is not "worlds," but "ages." "By faith we understand that the ages have been framed by the word of God." The word refers to a time element, not to a material structure. It does not refer to the cosmos materially, but to the passing of time, the passing of ages.

Here, then, the writer says that by faith we understand that the ages were framed by the word of God. At the beginning of this letter the writer says: "God . . . hath spoken unto us in His Son . . . through Whom also He made the worlds." There is the same mistake. It is "through Whom He fashioned the ages." The declaration of the writer, here, is that by faith we understand those periods, as they come and go, do not arise out of circumstances which cannot finally explain any age.

These changes in translation are of supreme importance to the true view-point of the great declaration made here by the writer. Let us now take those two declarations and consider them.

The writer first said, Faith is the attitude which has made possible the reception of a revelation, and so witness was borne. Through faith the elders gained, obtained news, a report, a statement, a revelation. Yes, in that sense faith obtained it, but they obtained it through faith. At once we are brought face to face with the philosophy of the passing of time, and the passing of every age; and also with the method by which we have obtained the statement found in Holy Writ. It is that statement which makes us still believe in Genesis, in spite of all criticism of Genesis. These elders obtained a report, they had a revelation. They were told how, in and through faith, the revelation came.

What was faith in their case? It was an activity which ceased speculation, and found God, an activity that was no longer content to examine events and circumstances and matter and material. That activity may be perfectly right in its place. But this was an activity which was no longer content to dissolve the earth and universe into their component parts, and then taking some component part, again dissolve it. This was not the activity that knocked at one door of the atom only, revealing each secret force vibrant with motion. They were men who turned aside from this, and said, When we have discovered the constituent parts of the universe, and the mystery of every particle of that universe; and have discovered the mystery; when we stand confronted with that which baffles us, we are touching God. Because they passed from the realm of speculation into the realm of listening, the writer could speak of them and say that they had obtained a good report. They obtained an account of the nature of man. They obtained a revelation of the method of Divine government. They obtained an interpretation that ever grew through the passing of those very ages into clearer showing of the nature and character of God. The nature and character of God were never discovered by speculation. We cannot discover any emotion by speculation or investigation. The mystery of law and government wraps us round everywhere. Not by investigation, but by faith we know; and faith obtains a good report. To that attitude God can speak.

The word "elders" here is synonymous with the word "fathers" in the first chapter. We could translate in our language "presbyter." In the past God spoke to the fathers, the elders, in divers portions and manners. They were men of faith, who came to the conclusion that nothing can be finally explained until God is found. By faith in God they obtained a good report, witness was borne.

Take the other declaration, "By faith we understand." What do we understand? We understand that the things seen "hath not been made out of things which do appear." By faith we understand that these ages have been framed by the word of God. "By faith we understand." We remember Tennyson's line,

"We have but faith; we cannot know."

I believe that to be entirely untrue. The truth is we now have faith, and so can know. That is a very different thing. That is what this writer says, "By faith we understand." That word "understand" simply means we exercise the mind. The mind may be exercised with God shut out, but no discovery is made as to the secret of the universe, or the character of God, or the nature of man. But by faith we understand. Faith is apprehension. It is the rational attitude of the soul. When faith has found God it has found the realm of reason. Faith is never credulity. "By faith

we understand." Faith appeals to the intelligence. Faith inter-
prets, and so we understand.

What is it we understand? I come back to the word so full of
significance. "By faith we understand that the ages have been
framed by the word of God." This is a most stupendous statement.
What are the ages? Periods of time, and they are always unlimited.
An age does not necessarily mean a certain period of time. It is an
interesting and revealing study in scientific investigation to read
about the Stone age, and the Bronze age, and the Iron age. They
are supposed to have succeeded each other, and very likely that is
true. There was the early age, the Stone age, when men began
out of the rocks to make weapons and tools, and so use the stones.
That age had its period, how long we do not know; and it was
succeeded by the Bronze age, when metals began to be understood
and intermixed, so that better tools and instruments were made.
Then came the most cruel and hardest age in human history, the
Iron age.

Again, I take up my Bible and see there the ages. The Stone
age, the geological age of Stone. There the mind of man was
working on the material, and there came the dawning of understanding in him. God was fashioning the age, whether it be of
stone, or of bronze, or of iron. I stand behind this Book, this
marvellous and miraculous Literature, and glance at the ages. There
are ages, some longer and some shorter. Let us summarise them.
There was the age of Innocence. Then sin entered, and there
followed the age of Conscience. That broke down and failed, and
there broke the age inaugurated by the call of Abram, the age of
Faith. That ran on over centuries, and when that was failing
another age dawned, the age of Law, which continued until Christ
came. That is the meaning of that New Testament word that the
law was our schoolmaster to bring us to Christ. Rather, it was our
guardian, our custodian. The law took us into custody. The
nearest approach to the Greek word there is the word pedagogue.
In the olden day he was the guardian, who saw that the boy attended
the lessons of his teacher, and looked after him. The nearest
approach to the pedagogue of the Greek time is the tutor at our
Universities. He does not teach, but is watching over students,
advising them what lectures to take, and seeing that they attend—
at least, he tries to do so! In that sense the law was our custodian
until Christ.

The age of the Christ lasted thirty-three years, just a generation
in human history. Then, the age of the Spirit. We are living

now in that age. We might correctly call it the age of the Church, for the Church is the body through whom the Spirit works. We might call it the age of Grace.

But there is another age, the age of Consummation, or the Golden age. Here they pass before us in this Biblical literature, the differing ages. By faith, the activity of our mind convinces us that God arranged all these ages; indeed He has framed them, He has fashioned them. The word "framed" may correctly be rendered fashioned completely by the word of God. Here "the word of God" is not the word *logos*, but *rhemati*—a fiat. God commanded, God ordained, God said, "Let there be," and there was. In the restoration of order seen in Genesis, He was commanding; and no word of God lacks power. Through all these running ages as they come and go, change and pass, the ultimate interpretation of every age is God.

Some may say to me: Are you not putting a lot of blame on God? There have been ages characterised by the uttermost cruelty, and you say that God framed them? Certainly, but that needs to be taken a step further. Look over the field of history from this standpoint, and we should remember there are certain facts that stand out clearly revealed. The first is this. Confining ourselves to the history of this Literature, all history reveals the faithfulness of God to His own creation in the freedom of human will. God is seen here, but I read through, and watch, and I see the human will is free, free to obey, free to disobey. God has created man, and has so fashioned the ages that they revolve around that central and marvellous mystery of the human will, with power to choose and elect. But God is revealed.

The second thought revealed is that of the maintenance of the authority of God as symbolized in the Garden of Eden at the beginning. Man was put into the Garden, and two things were said to him. "Thou mayest" and "Thou shalt not." "Thou mayest freely eat of every tree of the garden." It is the great charter of freedom. Thou shalt not eat of this one tree. That is the word that marks limitation and restriction of liberty, under the authority of God. God has never abandoned man. It has been true in all history and of the human race. Man has been free to obey or to disobey; to recognize or to rebel; but we have never been away from His authority.

That leads us a step further. The choices of humanity are worked out always to their logical conclusion, because this is a moral universe. It is in that fact that this is a moral universe that we recognise the government of God. He has fashioned the ages. He is always there. We cannot escape Him in any realm. Break a law, any law—I do not mean necessarily the Decalogue, or even the Sermon on the Mount—break law, and we have smashed God's universe. God is for evermore seen reigning, ruling. All human disaster is the result of human choice, worked out to its necessary issue. It is this compelling force of God's order that is making it so. God fashions the ages, but we are free. We can, if we like, take a philosophy that says that the ideals of Christ are the ideals of weakness. Such choose deliberately, and throw overboard the Man of Nazareth, and substitute the man of the mailed fist. Such teaching of the human race permeates the whole of it.

I speak now with reverence. Says God: Very well, you are free; but remember this, that your choice will work itself out to a harvest which is inherent in your choice. One harvest came in 1914, and the misery and muck of war was due to a philosophy that had turned its back upon Christ. That philosophy permeated us here in England, and we hugged it. There was a period when even theologians were not considered to be perfectly prepared for their work unless they had had a final year in the country that supported this philosophy. It goes on, and it works out in that way, because God is there, and He has created a moral universe in which man is free within limits; and the freedom of the will at last works out to the inevitable conclusion of the thing chosen, and that because God is governing.

That is the conviction of faith, and it is that confidence in the unseen that gives us conviction concerning things hoped for. We cannot escape Browning at this point:

> "That, after Last, returns the First;
>   Though a wide compass round be fetched;
> That what began best, can't end worst,
>   Nor what God blessed once, prove accurst."

In every age, as it succeeds, God is in it, moulding it, and allowing man his choice; but so shutting him in to the moral of eternal principles that at last his choice, whether for good or evil, comes to the harvest. "Be not deceived, God is not mocked; for whatsoever a man," or a nation, "soweth, that shall he also reap."

Yet the last thing to say in this connection is this. All history shows—and this is the marvel of it—God is making possible recovery, in spite of pain. There is always a second chance. There are always forces available to humanity, wherein and whereby humanity may turn in repentance, and find recovery and grace, and so be enabled to move forward. It is the very fashioning of the passing ages that they are for evermore moving on toward that final age when that rule and reign shall be acknowledged, and when the knowledge of the Lord shall cover the earth as the waters cover the sea.

V

The Faith of Abel

SCRIPTURE LESSON - - - - - - - Genesis iv. 1-16

"By faith Abel offered unto God a more excellent sacrifice than Cain, through which he had witness borne to him that he was righteous. God bearing witness in respect of his gifts; and through it he being dead yet speaketh" - - - - Hebrews xi. 4

FAITH has already been defined by the writer of this letter as to conduct; "My righteous one shall live by faith." It has been defined also as consciousness, "Faith is the confidence of things hoped for," based upon "conviction of things unseen." Moreover, we have considered what may be described as the creed of faith. "God is," and "He is a Rewarder" of such as "diligently seek after Him."

In illustrating the victories of faith the writer has declared it to be the origin of the records. Faith received a good report, and had witness borne to it concerning the will of God. Moreover, he has declared that by faith is discovered the ultimate truth concerning human history, the ages.

Turning then to the stream of human history, he selected illustrations of the power of faith. He began with Abel, and ended with Jesus.

The story behind the particular reference to Abel is recorded in Genesis iv, and is very familiar. Our Lord referred to him and to his death, "The blood of righteous Abel." This writer names him as a man of faith, and of that faith he tells us two things. First, by faith he offered to God an excellent sacrifice, which was accepted; and secondly, by faith "he being dead yet speaketh." These two things are distinct, yet closely related. Going back to the record of this man Abel, the writer declared that by faith he worshipped; secondly, that through faith "he being dead yet speaketh."

It is interesting that when this writer begins to illustrate faith he commences with a man at worship. There may be some significance in that. He did not mention Adam, and his faith, or Eve. He began with a man at worship and a member of a fallen race. There is no question about our first parents having faith in God,

34

either before they fell from their high estate, or after they had fallen, and God had talked with them. Here, however, is a son of the race, fallen; and he is seen at worship. That in itself is significant. An illustration of faith is given, faith being a principle in worship. Worship is the highest function of human life. Of man God said, "Whom I have created for My glory"; and all through the sacred Writings and through the experience of the Church man reaches the highest possible level of personality and possibility when he worships, not when he is working.

Here a man is seen at worship. Notice first of all the words, "Abel offered unto God." The word "offered" literally means *bore*, bore toward God, carried into God's presence. This indicates at once an attitude of the activity of worship. We may wonder where the place of worship was, for there was no Tabernacle erected, no Temple structure. Here we are back with primitive humanity. Where was the place of worship? There certainly was one, and these two brothers came to it, and brought their gifts into the presence of God. These are questions we ask, and cannot answer; but we are allowed, reverently, to speculate. I believe the place of worship at the beginning was at the gates of Eden, where cherubim guarded the entrance, man having been by his failure excluded by an act of God. The gates were the gates of exclusion.

This guarding by the cherubim is at least suggestive that it was at these very gates men came to worship. It is interesting to notice that "cherubim" guarded the gates of Eden, not seraphim. There is a difference clearly marked. A study of the words will show that cherubim were associated with Eden, the Tabernacle, the Temple, and the Throne of God. In every case the central idea is that of the Divine Presence, and the cherubim there to guard it. I think, therefore, that these two men in company probably with Adam and Eve, personally had a place of worship where the glory of the cherubim was shining at the very gates of the garden from which they had been excluded. Outside the garden, yet in worship they were drawing near, coming to the threshold, and so coming into the presence of God.

They are seen coming, and offering their gifts in sacrifice. Let us fasten our attention at once upon the gifts of these men. We are told Abel offered by faith "the firstlings of his flock and the fat thereof." That is the story as stated, which means that he brought to the place of worship offerings that had been slain. Death was there. Death was acknowledged. Not so with Cain. When he brought gifts they were vegetables, beautiful gifts from the ground, but there was no element of death, no suggestion of blood. Abel brought gifts that had been slain.

Here again we are in the realm of speculation. In these brief records, however, there are many things we are told because they are of value to us. There is no doubt that this first man and woman had received instructions from God to go to a place that God created and provided for them, and that when they had fallen, with infinite justice He talked to the woman, the man, and the serpent; and uttered that great promise that the seed of the woman should bruise the serpent's head. When her firstborn came, unquestionably she hoped that promise had been fulfilled, and she said, "I have gotten a man with the help of the Lord," who shall bruise the serpent's head. Then I think she very soon saw that her firstborn child was not destined to fulfil the great promise of the ideal of God, and in disappointed womanhood she named her second son Abel— Vanity. Her first cry, "I have gotten a man"; secondly, no, it was "Vanity," disappointment! After the forbidden act, when they clothed themselves with fig-leaves because they were naked and ashamed, God made them coverings, "coats of skin." We cannot read that without seeing behind those coats there had been sacrifice, death. I seem therefore to see behind that fact some instruction had been given, some method declared, some way indicated by which they were told to make to the place of the gates from which garden God had excluded them, by reason of the fact that they had excluded Him.

We are distinctly told, both in Genesis and in Hebrews, that God accepted Abel's sacrifice, and He did not accept the sacrifice of Cain. This is an old question, and has often been asked. Why did God accept one and not the other? There is only one answer that can be full and final. The sacrifice that Abel brought was a confession of sin, demanding sacrifice. There is no suggestion of sin in Cain's offering, no demand for sacrifice. When Abel came into the presence of God, bringing a sacrifice, this was the sign and acknowledgment of sin, and the need for some mediation in drawing nigh to God.

He was drawing nigh to God, to use a familiar word, but breaking it up into a word of three syllables, by at-one-ment. That is what atonement means, some method by which there can be atonement made for sin; the coming back of the sinner into the place of acceptance with God. The instructions for bringing a gift that marked a necessity for atonement was faith; faith not in man, but in God; and faith in God in two ways. First in His holiness.

There is no reference suggesting any conviction of the holiness of
God in what Cain brought; but Abel came with a blood offering,
and in doing so he was recognizing the holiness of God. But also
faith in the mercy of God. Knowing His holiness, and hoping for
His mercy, believing it on the basis of what He had already said to
the first woman, Abel drew near, and his offering said: Thou art
holy, I am sinning; but Thou art all mercy. Let my gift speak for
me, and represent me in Thy presence.

It is not correct to say, whereas there is an element of truth in it,
that God refused Cain's gift, and therefore refused the man; or that
God accepted Abel's gift, and therefore accepted the man. The
truth must be put in a different way. God accepted the man Abel,
and therefore his gift. He refused the man Cain, and therefore his
gift. The gift of Cain was a revelation of the man, and the gift of
Abel was a revelation of the man. The one was refused because
of what he was, as expressed in his gift; one accepted because of
what he was in himself and expressed in his gift. That is what the
writer meant when he said, "By faith Abel offered unto God a
more excellent sacrifice than Cain, through which he had witness
borne to him that he was righteous." Abel was a sinning man,
and yet a man whose attitude to God was a true one, and whose
gift proved his sense of the necessity for forgiveness in order that
he might approach. That constituted his right to be spoken of as
righteous, "God bearing witness in respect of his gifts." So Abel
stands for evermore at the head of the long line of worshipping
men and women, a revelation of what worship ever ought to be.

I once heard Dr. Hutton say, when speaking of the possibility
of our having perfect confidence in God, that we should always
walk through life, metaphorically at least, with bowed heads as
those who know they are sinners, saved only by grace. Surely
that is the very essence of worship. To come stridently, and without reverence into the presence of God, imagining we can worship
Him through flowers and fruits, and things aesthetic, all the trivialities that are dying as we touch them, is to insult His holiness.
Worship demands the approach based upon sacrifice. The sinner
is so accepted. There must be some way of atonement, at-one-
ment; and through the way provided by sacrifice, which is only
the beginning.

This rule runs all through the literature of the rites and ceremonies of the priesthood, all going to prove its necessity. We may
as well take our courage in both hands and say at once, this is the
meaning of the Cross. We cannot worship, we can never come to

God to worship, save by the way of the Cross. But by the way of the Cross a great provision was made, atonement was made; and sin can be dealt with, and put away by a righteous God; and we may lift our faces and look into His face and call Him "Our Father." That is worship, and nothing else suffices, however æsthetically beautiful it may be, until we come with solemnity to Him as men and women whose only hope is the Cross of Christ.

Then the story tells us, secondly, that "Through faith, he being dead yet speaketh." That simply means that his offering, as an action of faith never ends, but goes on. A true action of faith always runs on beyond the lifetime of the one who acts in faith. He is still speaking, and the story of the man is eloquent. "He being dead yet speaketh."

What did Abel say? What is Abel saying? There seems to have been a general idea that what the writer meant when he said, "the blood of sprinkling," that is, the blood of Jesus, "speaketh better than that of Abel" was that the blood of Abel cried for vengeance. That is not so, in spite of some of our hymns that we sing. It is not true. Is that the meaning of this? Is that the message that Abel is still uttering, though he is dead? Is it a cry for vengeance? I do not believe it. Read again what God said to Cain about the speech of Abel's blood. "The voice of thy brother's blood crieth unto Me from the ground," from the red soil, the earth. What had it to say? The general interpretation is that the voice of the blood cried to God for vengeance. This has never been the nature or the desire of faith. Indeed, he was not asking for vengeance. The Hebrew word there is almost a terrible one. To translate literally: "The voice of thy brother's blood shrieketh, crieth." It is a word that marks agony, pain. Why? Because the earth had swallowed that blood; and now the blood was crying, screaming out of dire agony.

What was this blood? It was the direct result of sin, the result of rebellion against God. When Cain slew his brother, he did it because he was evil. In that act he expressed what sin really is. Finally, the same thing was expressed for ever by Jesus on His Cross. The blood of Abel was the result of sin, and it cried to God. The blood sounding in the ears of God was the agonized cry of humanity for some way of atonement and reconciliation; for some way of return to God. In the shedding of his blood there was being voiced in the listening ear of God the shriek, the scream, the agonized calling of humanity.

Here in the twelfth chapter of Hebrews, at verse 24, the writer says, referring to the blood of Abel, that the blood of Jesus speaks better things than that of Abel. The blood of Abel cried aloud from the ground for some method of salvation, for some method of setting right. It was the voice of dire calamity. The blood of Christ does not cry for it, but declares that the cry is answered, that the atonement is made, that the great sacrifice through which humanity may come to the gates of Eden and meet with the cherubim, and retire into the inner place, is made. The blood of Jesus declared the atonement made. The blood of Abel was the cry of necessity, the cry of need, the anguished cry of humanity excluded from God. The blood of Jesus tells that there is a way for men to rise, a way of entrance into the Holy Place, past all the gate-keepers, certainly of men, and also of angels, and of the cherubim. So an act of faith is perfected in itself.

We come back to the old story, and Abel is speaking still, speaking in blood shed by sin as it cries to God; speaking in the sacrifice with which to approach the holy God. So our worship must be of that nature for evermore, offered because the blood of Christ for ever affirms the rent veil, the way of access made open.

VI

The Faith of Enoch

SCRIPTURE LESSON - - - - - - Genesis v

"By faith Enoch was translated that he should not see death; and
he was not found, because God translated him; for before his
translation he had witness borne to him, that he had been well-
pleasing unto God, and without faith it is impossible to be well-
pleasing unto Him" - - - - Hebrews xi. 5, 6

That is the New Testament commentary on and the interpretation of an
Old Testament story.

"Enoch walked with God; and he was not, for God took him"
Genesis v. 24

THE New Testament statement may thus be paraphrased: By
faith Enoch pleased God, and therefore God translated him that
he should not see death.

The Old Testament story is characterised by direct simplicity,
and we will consider it as revealing the victory of faith in the man
Enoch. The Old Testament writer simply says that Enoch walked
with God, and he was not, for God took him. The New Testament
writer goes behind the statement of the actual walk of the man,
and tells us his secret, so that we may understand the story.

The chapter in which it occurs is a remarkable record, stretching
over human history for fifteen hundred years. It is a very commonplace story. Birth and burial, passion and pain, living and dying.
The whole chapter gives the lie to the devil's lie in its solemn
march. In the hour of temptation, to which humanity had yielded,
he had said: "Hath God said, Ye shall not eat of any tree of the
garden?" The answer given by the woman was not accurate.
We are almost sure to go wrong at the beginning if we parley with
the devil. She said: "Of the fruit of the trees of the garden we may
eat." That was correct. "But of the fruit of the tree which is in
the midst of the garden, God hath said, Ye shall not eat of it, neither
shall ye touch it." God had said nothing of the kind. It is a habit
to add something to the commandment of God, and then object
to it. God had said: "In the day that thou eatest thereof thou shalt
surely die." Satan said: "Ye shall not surely die." We turn over
then to this fifth chapter, and through it we hear a tolling of the
knell of death, "And he died . . . and he died . . . and he died." So

history moves on; and the lie of hell was contradicted in the process of the history.

Only once across the fifteen hundred years the bell did not toll. There was no booming of the bell of death. Once the recorder had to change his phrasing, and instead of telling the story of a man who lived and died, he told of a man who lived; but when he came to record the end of his life, he could not add "and he died." He had to say, "He was not, for God took him." Upon that piece of history from the Old Testament there flashes the light of the New Testament declaration, as we are told, "By faith he was translated," because he had pleased God. In that he was pleasing to God, "without faith it is impossible to be well-pleasing unto Him." We ask why is it that for once in the long and monotonous process of history of burial upon burial a man is said to have been translated. The answer is self-evident; it was because he walked with God.

That brief story of Enoch is wonderful. A change came over the manner of his life. We are told he lived for 65 years, and begat Methuselah. After the birth of the boy a change came, and from then to the end of his life it could not be said of him in the ordinary phrasing, that he lived. After he begat Methuselah he walked with God for 300 years. It is a fascinating story. How the change came about we are not told. It has been surmised that there came to him some revelation, given in the life of many a man after the birth of his child. It may be that he then saw the darkness of the surrounding ages, and looked on, and understood the Divine movement, and so began to live by walking with God.

Now the story of that life and its consummation is told in suggestive phrases. To these I would ask your attention; first, that Enoch walked with God; secondly, he was not, because God took him.

We begin with the simple statement concerning his life. "He walked with God." The Bible is characterised by the glory and brevity of many of its biographies. Take David, for instance. It is a wonderful story in the historical section of the Old Testament; but in the New Testament we have the whole story summarised. "David, after he had in his own generation served the counsel of God, fell on sleep." That is a brief and full biography. Or to come to the biography of Saul: "I have played the fool." That is his story from first to last. But in all these biographical sketches none is more eloquent or more simply suggestive than this: "He walked with God."

What does it mean? What does it mean when we say we walk with anyone? We all know. What does walking mean? I will suggest four things of the simplest nature, and they apply perfectly to this story, and to this revelation of what life means when it is lived by faith. If a man walks with God, it means first, he moves in the Divine direction. Secondly, it means he is in agreement with God. Thirdly, it means there is mutual trust. Here a man trusted God, and God trusted him. Finally, if a man walk with God, it means that he keeps step with God.

Let us test these simple things. You were going home, and walked with someone. What does that mean? You went the same way, and if you were in agreement, there was no controversy between you. Therefore you trusted each other, and you kept step. Oh, I have walked with people who did not think it mattered if they were in step with me or not. They were making a great mistake. To one who loves music, the perfection of walking means rhythm, keeping in step, one step at a time.

Enoch walked with God, and that means he moved under the Divine direction. We are at once face to face with a question which will inevitably arise. In what sense can we speak of God as going anywhere? How can God decide the walk? A simple outlook upon all the history of humanity will at least bear me out when I say that nothing yet has reached finality. It is true of the whole creation of God, and of all human history. Everything is in a state of transition. As Tennyson has put it:

"Through the ages,
One increasing purpose runs."

But it runs; nothing is final and settled. With profound reverence, and yet with assurance, I declare that this is true about God, not about Himself, His own Being, but about His relation to His creation; and in His relation to humanity, and to human history. Everything is moving, in a state of transition, and God is moving in these things. Nothing is final. Nothing is complete.

What has been the line of the Divine going in human history? His going is that of uncompromising, unceasing, and unabating hostility to sin. That is the result of what God is in essence. The deepest fact concerning His Being is that He is love. That creates His unswerving hostility to sin in every form, because sin mars and ruins and blights and blasts His humanity. Whether we take the history of this Book, or go outside it, wherever we look, God is marching to war, a war with sin. He is out on a great campaign, and His campaign is fighting evil in every form. This is the necessity of the love of His heart.

In the thirty-third chapter of Isaiah the question is asked: "Who among us shall dwell with the devouring fire? Who among us shall dwell with everlasting burnings?" The presence of God is everywhere, and at all times, in all human history; it is devouring and blasting. It is an everlasting burning. The prophet asked the question: Who can dwell and live there? The answer is: "He that walketh righteously, and speaketh uprightly; he that despiseth the gain of oppressions, that shaketh his hands from holding of bribes, that stoppeth his ears from hearing of blood, and shutteth his eyes from looking upon evil." God's fire is for ever burning in wrath against evil, because evil blinds and blights and blasts humanity.

Enoch walked with God. From the moment of the birth of his child he did not live an ordinary life. His life was different, marked out from the ordinary life of the men and women surrounding him. He was marching with God in hostility to evil. He walked with God by faith.

But there is a deeper note. This means there was perfect agreement. That is not always included in walking with God. Some people who are in agreement with the general principle about God's purpose, and desire and action, are nevertheless not at peace with Him within their own lives. Agreement means the end of controversy, that a man shall not for a single moment oppose his will or opinion to the will of his God. Many people perceive the great Divine movement, and agree with it, even go so far as to utter its praise, and yet by some small controversy they are not in agreement with God, and are walking with God with their faces set toward the light, agreeing with His purpose. To make a modern application of this. There are many who praise and exult in the Sermon on the Mount, but they are not living by it. They agree that the Divine direction is the true one, but they are not walking with God, because there is still remaining a controversy between God and themselves. Whereas they may even be followers, they are not with Him. Enoch walked with God for 300 years. There was no controversy; and he was bound in all his life with the purpose, the passion, and the power of God. He walked with God.

That leads to mutual trust. To me that is a very arresting thought. Enoch trusted God about himself, as to all the ultimate issue of human history and human life. He trusted Him. That is why he walked with Him.

It is equally true that God trusted Enoch. God is speaking

to another man, Abraham: "Shall I hide from Abraham that which I do . . . for I have known him." Enoch trusted Him. "The secret of the Lord is with them that fear Him." What a marvellous declaration is made concerning Moses, which stands in terrible contrast to the next sentence:

> "He made known His ways unto Moses,
> His acts unto the children of Israel."

The children of Israel had to wait and see what He did. Moses was told beforehand. Because He trusted him, He could not hide His purpose, and talked with him face to face. And He trusted Enoch for 300 years. They moved in the same direction, in perfect agreement, trusting each other.

We come to perhaps the simplest, and yet the most acid test. For 300 years Enoch kept step with God, which simply means that he did not run before God, nor lag behind. Those are two things we are all so apt to do. How often zeal outruns knowledge, and we rush ahead with calamitous results. Then at other times zeal is absent, though knowledge is there, because the command puzzles us, and we lag behind. That is not perfect walking with God.

The supreme illustration of this point is that of Peter. In the dark night of betrayal, in the Garden, he ran ahead of his Lord, and drew his sword, and struck off Malchus' ear. That is zeal without knowledge. He was running ahead. He was not waiting for commands. He was not obedient to the will of his Lord. With fine heroism, as it appeared, he struck a blow, and the result was a poor business, for he only knocked off a man's ear! He might have struck off his head, not his ear. But zeal without knowledge met with a sharp rebuke: "Put up the sword into the sheath," "for all they that take the sword shall perish with the sword." From that moment Peter was offended, he felt he had been snubbed. Then what happened? He dropped behind, and followed afar off, and that lagging left him inside the gates, there by the fire with the enemies of Christ. First, heroic zeal! Now he is cursing and swearing, and insisting that he never knew Him! Running ahead, lagging behind! That is not walking with God. Walking with God is keeping step with God. The man who walks with God will not undertake any business until he knows the will of God. As James has put it: "Ye ought to say, If the Lord will, we shall both live, and do this or that." We used to say, God willing, but that is now out of date.

The other peril is that of lagging behind when He commands

the movement. We may run away, listening to the siren voices, and allow them to gain the victory; and we are left behind, until, perchance, we find ourselves getting warmth from the cold of the night at the fire of His enemies, and we shall say we never knew Him.

A man who walks with God will not run ahead or lag behind, but will keep step all the way. That is possible by faith, and faith only. There is no finer ideal of life than this. It may be objected that we are far advanced from the day of Enoch; that he lived in primitive times, not characterised by our complex age; that it was a much simpler thing to walk with God then than it could be now. Read again that fifth chapter of Genesis; and in the previous chapter there is the record of a race of men descended from Cain, and the culmination of the race in the seventh generation from Cain, in Lamech. Enoch was the seventh generation from Seth. Go back to the conditions of life in that generation in the midst of which Enoch lived. It was a generation of singularly prosperous humanity, on the human level. We find many interesting things. Lamech had several sons. One of them was Jabal, "the father of such as dwell in tents and have cattle." Another was Jubal, "the father of all such as handle the harp and pipe." Tubal-Cain was a great worker in metal. At that period under Lamech there was abuse and godlessness, and independence of control. These conditions existed when Enoch walked with God. The times are no more difficult to-day. Then, so now, mankind is remarkably successful, in spite of rebellion against God. Man is going on in his cleverness, with his music and mechanical contrivances; and never more so than to-day; and all the while singing a song of blasphemy against a holy God. Yet even in the midst of that, it is possible to walk with God, to move under the Divine direction, to be in agreement with God, to trust and know Him; going step by step, waiting for His movements and accompanying Him therein. This is the life possible to faith. But without faith, as the writer has said, "it is impossible to be well-pleasing unto Him."

How far are we walking with God? Many have their faces in the Divine direction, and are striving to end the controversy and are trusting Him. And God is trusting such, and marvellously trusting them. Are we keeping step with Him? If so, it is by faith. That is the finest biography that can be written.

Enoch was translated, that he might not see death. When taken from the earthly scene into the life beyond, it was not through the common gateway of death. Some may say that has no applica-

tion therefore to us. I am not sure. It may have a literal application
to some of us; for in the hour that He shall come, we that are alive
and remain, as the apostle tells us, shall be caught up to meet Him
in the air. There may be a great translation for some.

But is there not something more here? Is it not true that in
this Christian dispensation, Christians never see death? Jesus said:
"He that believeth on Me, though he die, yet shall he live; and who-
soever liveth and believeth on Me shall never die." All down these
Christian centuries the great procession has moved on, men and
women walking with God. Yes; they have died in our common
acceptance of the term, and yet in the larger and truer outlook not
one of them died. We still speak of "the swellings of Jordan" as
if they represented death; as though it was a cold river which we
have to cross. It is nothing of the kind. That is the outlook of
those left behind here; but the spirit, ransomed, realises his translation into the presence of God. What Mrs. Hemans sang about the
slave that lay dead in the Georgia rice fields, is true, namely, that
the body is "A worn-out fetter which the soul has broken and
flung away." So in the deepest fact of life, whenever a man walks
with God, at the end God receives him.

As we have seen the harmony of Enoch's life, notice the ending.
Enoch "was not, for God took him"; took him into partnership,
into fellowship, walked with him through all the vicissitudes of the
commonplace life, and then at the end gathered him home, that
he should not see death. I love the story of the little girl's outlook,
when she went home from Sunday School, after hearing the story of
Enoch. She said: "Mother, we heard about a wonderful man
to-day in Sunday School." The sensible mother let her child tell
what she had heard. "His name was Enoch, and you know, Mother,
he used to go for walks with God." The mother said to her:
"That is wonderful, dear. How did it end?" "Oh, Mother, one
day they walked on and on, and got so far, God said to Enoch,
'You are a long way from home. You had better come in and stay
with Me!'"

God has been saying that to our loved ones again and again.
They have gone in to stay with Him, with Whom they had walked
their earthly pilgrimage.

VII

The Faith of Noah

SCRIPTURE LESSON - - - Genesis vi. 5-14, 22, and vii. 5

"By faith Noah, being warned of God concerning things not
seen as yet, moved with godly fear, prepared an ark to the saving
of his house; through which he condemned the world, and
became heir of the righteousness which is according to faith"

Hebrews xi. 7

TAKEN as an illustration of faith, the story of Noah is remarkable, and indeed, unique. In it faith is revealed, acting on the same
principles as in other cases, but in unexampled circumstances. I
propose that in considering this text we should consider first the
man and the times in which he lived; and then attempt to understand something of the operation of his faith in those times.

How much do we really know about Noah? We know he
built an ark; and that he got drunk; and that often exhausts the
common knowledge of this man Noah. Nevertheless he stands
out as one of the most remarkable personalities on the page of the
Old Testament. He must be judged partly by the times in which
he lived, and finally by his action in those times.

Take first that story of his getting drunk. Some people seem
possessed with that fact, and do not think of him respectfully. But
read the story carefully. There is no proof that there was any sin
in the action. We are told he "was a husbandman and planted a
vineyard." Then we are told he drank of the wine, and was
drunk. Has it ever occurred to some that the drunkenness was an
accident? In the Hebrew Bible there are many words for wine.
Here this is the first occurrence of the Hebrew word Yayin, which
means simply and literally, intoxicating drink, the root of the
word having the thought of fermentation. The word here used
for his drinking is one of the intensive words. It simply means
to drink deeply. Now I very much doubt whether Noah knew the
effect it would produce upon him; and I am inclined to think this
is the first instance on record of a man taking intoxicating drink
and not knowing what effect it would have: and he became drunk.
Another word for this is equally correct, he became satiated. It

47

made him very sick. It was foolish, wrong, perhaps he should have known better. But there is no hint of moral delinquency here, when he did it.

What sort of a man was he? I repeat the Biblical description. "Noah was a righteous man and perfect in his generation." I would change that word "generation" for some other—perfect among his contemporaries. Then comes the summing up of the whole fact: "Noah walked with God." Here is the great fact of his life, and what a radiant revelation it is of a remarkable character, perfect among his contemporaries.

We had the same expression in our last study, on Enoch. "Enoch walked with God." It is arresting that of only two men in all Bible history is it declared that they walked with God. Here were two men, so distinctive that the recorder of olden time, referring to them, had to say that they walked with God. As we saw in our last study on Enoch, that meant that Noah moved in the same direction in which God was moving; and that he was in agreement with God, had no controversy on the way, moreover that they kept in step with one another. Enoch and Noah did not run before the Lord. They kept pace with Him. They did not lag behind the goings of God. They kept beside Him. God did not hurry ahead of Enoch and Noah. He adapted His goings to their possibilities. He never lagged behind, as they went forward. He was always with them.

Noah was the great-grandson of Enoch. Enoch begat Methuselah, and Methuselah begat Lamech, and Lamech begat Noah. We have a glimpse into conditions of the times as we read the names. When Noah was born, Lamech gave him the name which means comfort. That is a remarkable thing. We see the comfort that Lamech expected from this baby boy. Now we shall be set free from the curse that is on the soil. It was purely materialistic. He hoped that the child would grow up in his home, setting him free from the curse of the soil, and the toil necessary to the earning of bread with the sweat of his brow.

The recorder, telling the story of Noah, has said that he was a righteous man, perfect among his contemporaries; standing out, different from them, and afterwards summarised in that great statement that "Noah walked with God."

Let us look a little more closely at the text, in which this statement is made about him. "Being warned of God." That word *warned* has a profounder meaning than may appear on the surface. The Hebrew word is variously translated. The word simply means literally that God told him, admonished him, spoke to him, warned him. God revealed to this man a purpose.

Looking at Noah again, we see the motive of his life. It is declared that he was "moved with godly fear." The Authorised reading omits the word "godly." It is the Revised which correctly says, "moved with godly fear." Fear was the motive of his life as he walked with God. That is not fear that is slavish and terrifying; but the fear which is the fear of the Lord, and the beginning of wisdom. It refers to his awe in the presence and majesty of God, and to his urgent attempt to obey. That was the inspiring motive of what he did: "moved with godly fear." So we see him, not only walking, but talking with God, and listening to Him, passionately desiring one thing only, that is, the honour and glory of God.

So the man stands before us, limned in short, brief, pregnant sentences, revealed as one of the most remarkable and outstanding figures in Old Testament history.

With equal brevity, consider the times in which this man lived as they are revealed in the story, reading the story carefully.

Let us notice the description of the times. "The wickedness of man was great." That is a description of the human race at that time. That is not true to-day. The brief sentences are almost redundant in their employment of terms to reveal the depth of the depravity. "Every imagination of the thoughts of his heart was only evil continually." Have we ever sat down in front of that, and thought it out? Thoughts always act in the realm of the imagination. Every imagination, every vision, every thought, every conception, only evil; and that not on one day, but "continually"! That is a picture of the human race that is the most appalling possible. There is nothing in the literature of the Bible or outside it, which is so graphic, terrifying, and overwhelming as the revelation of what humanity was at that time. Mark the superlativeness of it all—"Every . . . only . . . continually . . . evil." Those were the times in which Noah lived, the characterisation of the contemporaries among whom he lived.

Our Lord referred to those times. He said, "In those days which were before the flood they were eating and drinking, marrying and giving in marriage." Everything was going on as usual. Indeed, if they had known the modern phrase, they might have used it—"Business as usual." On the ordinary level, they were progressing, and yet, every imagination of the thoughts of their hearts was evil continually. It is an appalling picture of the times.

But faithful Noah, being told of God of the things unseen, was

4

moved and inspired by godly fear to prepare an ark for the saving
of his house. Mark that carefully. There was no evidence of
the things God was telling him. They were things unseen. Mark
the operation of this man's faith. We have referred to it in connection with his life and conduct. He walked with God, and God
talked to him. He warned him, spoke to him, admonished him.
He was a lonely soul. Look round and see the condition of human
life all around him; yet in the midst of it all, he walked with God,
feared God, and was spoken to by God. Faith in God is seen
operating.

What was his consequent outlook? What did Noah see,
because he was walking by faith? There are two things I suggest.

First, he was conscious of that very evil in the midst of which
he was living. That consciousness of evil was born of his communion with a holy God. Evil is never seen, except from the standpoint of the Divine holiness, and the Divine insistence, and the
Divine requirements. Here was a man walking with God, com-
muning with God, fearing God, serving God. He saw the evil,
the corruption, and how terrible it was, because he lived in fellowship with God. That is always so with faith. Real faith never
thinks lightly of sin. Real faith never looks out upon conditions
of corruption as though they were evanescent, and did not very
much matter. That is how faith operated in Noah.

But I go further, and declare that in his case he was not only
conscious of evil, but he also had an understanding of the degrada-
tion of it. Faith gave him a conviction of the inevitability of the
Divine wrath. That was born of his knowledge, not of the holy
God merely, but of the righteousness of God and the ruling and
reigning of God. Noah knew what God told him was about to
happen. He felt the righteousness of it, the rectitude of it.

That brings us to the simple statement that by faith he built
his ark. Faith brought him into active co-operation with God in
His purpose and plans. Noah did not build that ark as the result
of what he could see. Men were eating and drinking, marrying
and giving in marriage, business was as usual; there was indifference
to the dereliction of the nation and the corruption of the race.

Noah and his three sons could never have built that ark with
their own hands. What became of the workmen who helped
them: those who prepared the gopher wood, fastened it together,
and carried out the instructions? As Jesus said, they were swept
away. They went on building the ark, and they were eating,
drinking, marrying, and carrying on their occupations. I have

no doubt they were laughed at for building the ark. What a stupid thing! What a ridiculous idea! For one hundred and twenty years Noah was preaching righteousness. They had not listened. They had not noticed. They had turned a deaf ear to the preaching, because they believed a madman was building the ark. When the flood came, the builders of the ark were swept away because of what they were in themselves, in spite of the fact that they had been workmen preparing that which was to be God's vantage ground for His movement in history.

That is a terrible thought. It reacts upon us. It may be possible to-day that we are helping to build the ark, and we are so busy here and there, doing all sorts of things that are contributory to the Divine purpose, and yet ourselves are corrupt, evil, every imagination of the thoughts of the heart only evil continually.

But Noah worked with God, as well as walked with God, in obedience and faith. Certainly in obedience he wrought to build the ark, and so he served in the carrying out of the Divine purpose.

Is there any application of this story to ourselves? That is a shattering question. Let it be admitted: never since that time has humanity sunk so low as this. Though there are some very dark and terrible things revealed in other periods in history in the Bible, and out of it, there is no description of a race having sunk so low that the recorder has to say that "Every imagination of the thoughts of his heart was only evil continually." Only evil, no gleam of light, no change of thought, rotten, evil continually. The human race has never sunk so low since. Why not? Because Noah built his ark; and the work of God has moved forward from that new beginning. Never again have men sunk as low as that. The elect remnant in that ark has prevented it sinking to such unutterable depths of depravity as existed before the flood.

But the same principle of evil is at work, and it has the same manifestations. Business is still as usual, eating and drinking, marrying and giving in marriage; busy about our work, and material things. The principle is still at work, and we see it everywhere.

And the same God is supreme. He has never been other than supreme. Consequently the same testimony to righteousness is necessary. This supreme illustration should warn and admonish us. In a day when the principle of evil is working, God is reigning; and He is always looking for Noah, for men and women to walk with Him, to fear Him, and obey Him; to do things that appear so utterly without reason when He commands them; to build an ark of gopher wood for the coming flood, when there is no sign of the flood! Men will laugh and mock if we do this kind of thing. Noah walked with God by faith. He carried on by faith. He did the thing for which he could see no reason except that God commanded him. He fell into line with the Divine order. He carried out the Divine instruction. He built his ark, and gave God His vantage ground for another movement in human history.

That is what He is wanting us to do: to witness by faith, when all things seem contradictory; when all the circumstances of the hour seem to show that the things we are doing are supremely futile. Believing in God, hearing His voice, believing His word, we march on; and by our obedience condemn the world; and carry on the great march of righteousness toward its consummation.

No; things have never been at such a low ebb as then. It was a low ebb when they put Jesus on His Cross. No, not racially. There was a small elect remnant then; and even there in the midst of the dense darkness, God was carrying on. He always marches through those who have heard Him, who are obedient to Him, and do His commands.

VIII

The Faith of Abraham

SCRIPTURE LESSON -　-　-　-　-　Hebrews xi. 8-19
"By faith Abraham, when he was called, obeyed" ·　　Heb. xi. 8
"By faith he became a sojourner in the land of promise" Heb. xi. 9
"By faith, Abraham, being tried, offered up Isaac"　　Heb. xi. 17

OF the greatness of Abraham there can be no question. He
is claimed by Mohammedanism, by Judaism, and by Christianity;
and is held in profound reverence in each case. Someone has taken
the trouble to go through the Koran, and has found that Abraham
is mentioned therein no less than 188 times. He stands out in
human history as one of the greatest personalities. It was of Abraham that James said, "he was called the friend of God." In the
Old Testament there are two occasions upon which he is so described: once by Jehoshaphat, when in an hour of danger he was
praying out of a full heart, and out of the sense of a deep necessity,
he spoke of Abraham, the founder of the race, and said: "Abraham,
Thy friend for ever." The other occasion is found in the prophecy
of Isaiah; when the prophet was declaring the message of God,
and repeating the words of Jehovah, he said, "Abraham, my
friend." Of no other man is it ever recorded in that way. Or
Moses it is said that he talked with God as a friend; but here this is
said of this one man, "the friend of God." I would not be misunderstood, for God has had His friends in all ages; but this is the
one outstanding occasion when the declaration is made, and cited
in the New Testament, thus corroborating the statement of the
Old, that Abraham was a friend of God.

In this classic passage on faith, the writer has more to record
about him than of any other. Beginning at verse eight, the story
continues, with some parenthetical interpretations to verse nineteen.
This, of course, is a condensed story, and any consideration of the
faith of Abraham must necessarily be a condensed consideration.
In the story there are three great movements referred to, and they
are indicated in the texts. They reveal a widening experience, or
rather, a deepening experience in the life of Abraham. First, faith

53

obeying: "By faith, Abraham, when he was called, obeyed." Faith, onlooking, sojourning in the land of promise, "by faith he became a sojourner in the land of promise." Faith offering: "By faith, Abraham, being tried, offered up Isaac." We may thus gather the whole story and consider the revelation of the force of faith in the life of this man Abraham.

Faith obeying. What is the background of the story? It is not here with any fulness. Even in the Old Testament record the references are slight, although very definite. It has been emphatically stated that this man Abraham never lived; that he was an eponymous hero, that he was an imaginary figure. By the same people it has been said that Moses could not possibly have written the Pentateuch, because writing was not known in his time. That is all past now, and the world has grown through that stage, for to-day we know that Abraham is a figure in the actual history, springing from Ur of the Chaldees. Archæological excavation has revealed to us Ur of the Chaldees, and has shown a remarkable condition of high material and mental civilization existing there in Ur. Small facts illustrate. Some time ago, in the midst of the excavations, they dug up the remains of a house in which was a clay tablet which had been left unfinished, and on that tablet, whoever had been using it, was the working out of a problem in trigonometry, which problem they are still working out at Oxford and Cambridge. So it was not a barbaric condition on which Abraham turned his back when he left Ur of the Chaldees, but a high form of civilization on the material and mental levels; without any evidence of anything in the nature of high spiritual or moral standards. That is Abraham's background, and it was there he heard the call. "Now Jehovah said unto Abram, Get thee out of thy country, and from thy kindred, and from thy father's house, unto the land that I will show thee: and I will make of thee a great nation, and I will bless thee, and make thy name great; and be thou a blessing; and I will bless them that bless thee, and him that curseth thee will I curse; and in thee shall all the families of the earth be blessed" (Gen. xii. 1-3). That was the call Abraham heard, a call to leave kith and kin and country, and all the conditions there, that ultimately by going from those conditions he might be a blessing to all the world.

Now obedience to that call was only possible to faith, and in the surrender to that call faith was operating. We may ask, How did he know it was God's voice speaking to him, as if he heard the voice of a friend, and not the voice of any Chaldean? I do not know, and I am not caring to know, or to find out. What I do know is that Abraham was convinced that the call had come to him to turn his back upon Ur, and that it was God's call. Of that he was perfectly sure. What processes of mind and thought in Abraham may have preceded this we can only infer. We can infer that he had come to an hour of disillusionment, of bitter dissatisfaction with life as it was being lived; and the order of life which is contrary to the high, and the noble and true. Somehow he had come to a consciousness of God, had come to know God; and there, in the midst of the conditions that obtained in Ur, he had known that it was God speaking to him. That one thing is certain, that a man knew God had spoken. When we see that, the wonder of his action fades away. It is the kind of action one would expect; yet it was only possible to faith.

In that twelfth chapter of Genesis, the next sentence we read is: "So Abram went out, as Jehovah had spoken unto him." In the Hebrews' reference, the writer says not only that he went out, but he did not know where he was going; but he is equally careful to say that though he did not know where he was going, he knew what he was going for, and why he was going. "He looked for the city which hath the foundations, whose Architect and Framer is God." But Ur had foundations? No, Ur had nothing but that which was material; and so evanescent was it that it was buried for long centuries in an accumulation of dust and rubbish. He sought a city that had foundations, whose order of life, Whose Architect and Builder was God Himself; and he went because God told him to go, and by faith he obeyed.

So we see faith obeying, a man going out to become a pilgrim and a stranger; going out to undertake a march without a map, on a progress without a programme, but going with God. That is the first element of faith in the man, and wonderful in itself. Application is hardly necessary. Can we get the vision this gives us, a man hearing God, hearing God's command to do a thing that seemed absurd? Yet that thought did not daunt him. He set up his standard of life, shook the dust of Ur from his feet, and went out on the march. Where? Never mind where, but go. No wonder he has been called the father of the faithful! That was a marvellous act of obedience.

We are apt to read the second text, and fail to notice that there is another element here. By faith he was able to obey, and by faith "he became a sojourner in the land of promise." Not a landowner, but dwelling in tents with Isaac and Jacob. We shall return to that reference to Isaac and Jacob later. Let us see Abraham, without a city, now become a sojourner. The idea of the word *sojourner* is arresting and suggestive. It is that of being a lodger, and not one owning the place. The word sojourner is a beautiful word, which we do not want to lose; but it means he was simply a lodger; a sojourner not in active possession.

How long did that last? By faith he became a sojourner, and he remained a sojourner. How long? Just about one hundred years. He was heir of the promise. His title was the word of God to him; but when he died, after being a lodger for a hundred years, how much did he possess of the land? Machpelah, the burying-place of Sarah. That was all, but he had faith, and he was content to wait. By faith he was a sojourner, and when the end came to his life on the earthly plane, all that he owned in that land was a cave in a field. That was all. Read that story, and see that he declined to take it as a gift from aliens. He bought it, and insisted upon paying for it; and the transaction was legally done, and he became the owner of a burying-ground. That is all that Abraham himself ever owned in the country; but by faith he was a sojourner.

I thank God that all these stories tell us the truth about these men, of failure as well as success. His was wonderful faith, but there were some sad deflections from faith in the early part. Abraham went down into Egypt, and we know of his trouble there, and the difficulty created. If the pagan Egyptian king had not had some sense of honour, there would have been a terrible catastrophe. He could not trust God wholly with his future. Yet follow the story through, and in those hundred years he obeyed, waiting, trusting. By faith he became a sojourner. He had turned his back upon a great city, a great civilization. He had gone out seeking a city whose Builder and Maker is God. He was seeking a country, a heavenly, when he was pitching his tent, and dwelling, a sojourner, under the oaks of Mamre. Cities there were full of material property and wealth; but Abraham was not lured by them. Lot was, and that was where Lot broke down. He was a good man, but he allowed himself to be seduced by the promise of a way by which wealth might be quickly accumulated. But Abraham sat under the oaks, unaffected by the lure of the cities. He accepted the unsettled life. He was a stranger and a pilgrim in the midst of things so contrary to vision that had come to him, and to the call he had heard. He was a pilgrim, travelling all the while. He

> "Nightly pitched his moving tent,
> A day's march nearer home,"

the city of his heart, the passion of his life. Faith manifested itself in the fact that he was a sojourner for a hundred years. Whatever the difficulties, he never went back to Ur.

So finally we come to that which is the climax and central fact. "By faith, Abraham, being tried, offered up Isaac." That does not necessarily refer to sacrifice by death. The word "offered" simply means he presented him, he yielded him to God. When God asked him to offer his son, he consented by faith, apparently sacrificing all his hopes. That is what this means. Apparently. That is how it looked. But Abraham did not measure things by the apparent way. He had waited long for Isaac, for a son; and the son had been given supernaturally. Isaac was born out of due season. He had seen this son grow up, at any rate at this time some thirty or forty years old; and he had to consent to the action of his father, which undoubtedly he did. When God said to Abraham, Give Me thy son, he yielded Isaac to Him in the only way he saw, and that was by putting him to death. So Abraham journeyed with him—and what a journey it was! When they neared the place of sacrifice, Abraham said to the men: "Abide ye here . . . and I and the lad will go yonder; and we will worship, and come again to you." He was going to offer Isaac, to the uttermost limit, even to death. Yet there was a confident assertion that that was not going to be the end. He was coming back and the lad was coming back with him. The father of the faithful!

What is the meaning of this? "By faith Abraham, being tried, offered up Isaac," though in him were vested all his hopes. He followed what seemed to him the only course, the only way in which he could present that lad to God, in answer to the Divine call. But he was "accounting," reckoning, reasoning that God was able to raise him up, even from the dead. That is what he meant when he said: "I and the lad will go yonder; and we will worship, and come again to you." He was willing to go to all lengths, and to slay him; and when the hour came he made the offering, reckoning that if he put Isaac to death, God would raise him up from the dead. The writer says: "From whence he did also in a parable receive him back." That is the central, most precious thing he did: yielding, accounting.

Faith is not blind unbelief. Faith is not superstition. Faith works by reason. It does the thing that seems contrary to expectation, but it does it, reckoning on God by faith, being sure of God; being sure that after Abraham had done his utmost, and his sun was blotted out of his heaven, God was able to raise Isaac up. By faith Abraham offered up his son. That was the supreme activity.

Faith is conviction of God, and that He is the Rewarder of them that diligently seek Him. This is wrought out all through the story of Abraham. As we watch faith in him we see it honoured by God, in spite of faltering, and in spite of failure. We see God over-ruling the failure in man, and bringing everything to consummation. We do not wonder that Abraham is called the father of the faithful. The phrase is not found in Scripture but the teaching of the New Testament warrants it.

In the days of His flesh His enemies said to Jesus, in answer to His word that "the truth shall make you free," "We be Abraham's seed, and have never yet been in bondage to any man; how sayest Thou, Ye shall be made free?" Our Lord said this startling thing: "I know that ye are Abraham's seed," but you are not his children. Mark that carefully. Only those who live by faith are the children of Abraham.

Paul said of Abraham, "who is the father of us all." He was writing to Christian people. So everyone to-day who believes, who lives by faith, and obeys when the call comes, waits, is content to make the offering God demands at whatever cost: such are the children of Abraham. Such are the souls who by their faith in God, become God's instruments through whom He hastens the day of faith's final victory.

IX

The Faith of Isaac

SCRIPTURE LESSON -   -   -   Genesis xxvii. 1-4 and 26-40
"By faith Isaac blessed Jacob and Esau, even concerning things
to come" -   -   -   -   -   -   Hebrews xi. 20

AFTER devoting two paragraphs to the faith of Abraham, the writer seems almost to dismiss the next three men, Isaac, Jacob, and Joseph. Yet that would not be a correct statement. He does not dismiss them, but names them, giving an account of the power of faith in their lives; referring to them as mountain peaks in the history of the Hebrew people. He makes no reference to them on their pilgrimage. In each case the illustration of faith comes on the border-line, when they had arrived at that period of life when a man inevitably looks across to the life that lies beyond, when a man is inevitably and happily conscious that he is at the end of his pilgrimage.

"By faith Isaac blessed Jacob and Esau even concerning things to come." When did he do this? When he was old. He had almost completely lost his sight, and was trembling on the verge of eternity. As we proceed we read:

"By faith Jacob, when he was dying, blessed each of the sons of Joseph"; and again:

"By faith Joseph, when his end was nigh, made mention of the departure of the children of Israel." It is arresting that these three illustrations are drawn from that period in life when a man is approaching the end and is looking on. The writer of this letter says that in that hour, approaching the end of the earthly pilgrimage, by faith Isaac, Jacob, and Joseph demonstrated their faith.

"By faith Isaac blessed Jacob and Esau, even concerning things to come." The text is arresting. The story to which it refers reflects no credit upon Isaac. Nevertheless in its entirety it is the supreme revelation of his faith. Whereas criticism has been made of his life, at the very last, when flesh was failing, and sight was dim, faith suddenly shone out; and the underlying principle of his life was manifest in that closing hour.

59

In looking at this story, we will consider first the man himself; then the account of his deterioration until he came to the sad condition seen in the 27th chapter of Genesis: finally leading us to the triumph of his faith. "By faith, Isaac blessed Jacob and Esau."

When we consider the man, there is not very much to be said about Isaac. He is certainly not an impressive character. As to temperament he was a man passive, rather than active. There is nothing in the story of his life that speaks of initiation, or of the nature of action. All the early triumphs he had were of a passive nature. If the triumph of faith is maintained, when he tramped the mountain of Moriah with Abraham, to be offered in sacrifice, we know there must have been consent on his part. We make a great mistake thinking of him then as a lad, a stripling, for Isaac was then about 33 years of age. He entered into his father's plan by faith, but he yielded himself. It was not an initiative action. It was passive faith.

Take the story of how he got his wife: there essentially he was passive. He had no choice in the matter, merely agreeing with the principle that he should not marry into the surrounding nations. By faith, and in agreement with that principle, he waited until Rebekah came. It is a beautiful story of how he went into the fields, lifted up his eyes, and beheld Rebekah. Going out, and finding her there, he accepted her. It was faith, but not adventurous faith.

Then of course, the supreme fact about Isaac that impresses us is that he dug wells, and kept on digging them. His quiet persistence in that action was part of his faith. When an enemy came and took possession of the wells, what did Isaac do? He dug another well. He did not grudge them the well. If that had happened to Abraham, he would have protested with righteous indignation. Jacob would have outwitted them, and had more wells than the enemy had taken from him before he had finished with them. But not so Isaac. He just went on digging. Yes, he was a quiet man, a passive man rather than active; and the demonstration of faith recorded here in Hebrews does not refer to any of these matters. It has to do wholly with the events in which the fundamental principle overcame certain actions which had violated even the principle of faith. In the presence of that violation, faith asserted itself with great strength and magnificence.

Then look at the man and mark the story of his deterioration. Evidently he had become by this time a man largely flesh-governed. In all probability that was due to his passivity, that he had yielded himself to that passive state, without trying to make any deliberate effort. When life is never active, in the true sense of the word venturesome, it is always in danger. So it was with Isaac. Reading the story we see he loved Esau. Why? Because he fed him. That is a blunt way of putting it, but it is plainly recorded. Esau fed him, and Isaac loved his venison.

The deterioration of the man is evident in the matter of the blessing. He pronounced the father's blessing upon the son, but it was under fleshly inspiration that he did it. He wanted the meal first, and then the blessing. We note these things because they lead on to the final matter of the blessing. He made a deliberate attempt to change the purpose of God from the instrument through whom it had been clearly revealed to him, God would carry out that purpose. At the birth of the twins it was made known to him that the Divine activity would be carried on through Jacob, and not through Esau. It was one of those occasions, of which there are many more in Biblical history, that show that in the economy of God the eldest son necessarily being the heir, has no place. The choice was based upon something far deeper. It had been made, and Rebekah and Isaac knew of it, and knew all the way through that the blessing, the patriarchal blessing, which in the last analysis was the blessing of God, should rest upon Jacob, chosen to carry out the purposes of God. Isaac in his deterioration still believed in the purposes of God, and that those purposes should be carried out; yet he determined to deflect the blessing from the one God had appointed to the man who had pandered to his weaknesses. There was nothing of faith in that, rather the violation of the principle.

How then was that triumph of faith manifested? First in the actual words of the blessing. Every word is descriptive, and every sentence in that blessing proves the recognition of God. Faith is manifest in the blessing that Isaac uttered. The fact that when he uttered the words of blessing which fell on Jacob, he imagined that he was speaking to Esau, reveals a failure, not a triumph of faith. But faith insisted upon the fulfilment of a Divine purpose through his seed, even though it attempted in its folly to change the channel. He was trying to alter the method, but he was not trying to alter the purpose.

Then comes the remarkable fact, that here faith shines out most clearly, when he found how he had been tricked. The trickery of man had wrought in the interest—curiously, marvellously enough—of the purpose of God. Isaac had attempted by his stupid cleverness and lustful desire to fasten the blessing upon one man not God-appointed; and he found that he had failed, and that the blessing had fallen upon the God-appointed man. We see him then accepting the interference of God, after his foolish plan had been set aside and refused, and the blessing was pronounced upon Jacob.

In the twelfth chapter of Hebrews, at verse 16, we read: "Esau, who for one mess of pottage sold his own birthright. For ye know that even when he afterwards desired to inherit the blessing, he was rejected (for he found no place of repentance) though he sought it diligently with tears." That does not mean that he did not repent, but that he could not make his father repent, though he sought to do so with tears. The old man, feeble, ashamed, knowing he had played the fool and had attempted to play a trick on God, which trick having been invalidated by another trick, God was vindicated; when he found that was so, he would not withdraw that blessing. He stood by it. "By faith Isaac blessed Jacob and Esau." Faith insisted upon the fulfilment of the Divine purpose, even though it had attempted in its folly to change the channel of faith. Faith recognized the failure and the wrong of what it had done, and when God had overwhelmed it, would not stay the blessing.

As we ponder this story, how true it is that sometimes the deepest faith a man has in God is seen in his attitude toward his own wrong-doing. That was the deepest fact in Isaac; that faith in the God of his father Abraham, that faith that had been the inspiration of his quiet, passive life, and that faith that prevailed after all. He attempted to change the Divine purpose as declared to him, but faith nevertheless was the greatest thing in his personality. We see it plainly in his attitude resulting from his failure, when he stood rebuked in the presence of the purpose of God, and the God of purpose. This is often so. It was so in the case of David. It was never more completely revealed than in the attitude he took up, after his outstanding sin. It was so in the case of Peter. He cursed and swore that he did not know Jesus. But watch him, see that breaking heart, and watch all that followed after. Out of absolute failure, resulting from a failure of faith, at last faith burned brightly and triumphed.

We may be inclined to say that Isaac was in every way weak, yet the writer of this letter does not omit him. Thus we have an instance of how deeply embedded the principle of faith may be, and how it triumphs eventually over personal weakness.

What a wonderful word that is that God spoke to His people on their pilgrimage in Exodus. "I am the God of Abraham, and of Isaac, and of Jacob." That becomes more radiantly wonderful when we remember that our Lord Himself quoted those very words as Matthew records. He said: "He is the God of Abraham, and of Isaac, and of Jacob. He is not the God of the dead but of the living." We are not now concerned with the application that our Lord made of that, but we are concerned with that statement made by Jehovah, and reaffirmed by Jesus. "The God of Abraham"; yes, we can understand that. "And of Isaac"? We might not have thought so, but God did. He is the God of Isaac. "And Jacob." Perhaps we think less of him than of Isaac; but God has linked him up in the great statement to the nation. "I am the God of Abraham, of Isaac, and of Jacob." Oh, the honour of it! If a man has failed, Abraham might not have been of very much help to such an one. But we see a weak man, and a clever, tricky man; and have heard God say that He was the God of the three. So He is the God of every man who has faith in Him, however much he may falter, however much he fails. Whenever a man has faith, sooner or later, even though it falter, faith will be seen in its true perspective, and it will surely triumph, and manifest itself in love.

X

The Faith of Jacob

SCRIPTURE LESSON - - - - - - Genesis xlviii

"By faith Jacob, when he was a-dying, blessed each of the sons
of Joseph; and worshipped, leaning upon the top of his staff"
—Hebrews xi. 21

WE have in succession three stories of faith operating at the
end of life; Isaac blessed Jacob and Esau; now Jacob blessing
Ephraim and Manasseh; and in the next story, the faith of Joseph
at the end.

In the case of Jacob we have another arresting method implied
by the writer of the letter in proof of his faith. All the earlier
stories of his life are omitted, and we see him at the end, when he
was a-dying, his eyes dim, and he was leaning in his weakness
upon his staff, when he had to make an effort to sit up, when
Joseph brought his two boys to him. He was an old man, and withal
a dying man.

He had come to that hour in which all the past is seen in its true
perspective. The writer takes what he did in that hour as demon-
strating his faith, and unquestionably it is a remarkable story. In
human feebleness, leaning upon the top of his staff, he worshipped.
Do not omit that. He did not only bless the sons of Joseph, but he
worshipped by faith in that hour; and in that attitude of worship he
pronounced a blessing upon those two sons of Joseph.

To understand all this we need to see the man, and to consider
the terms of the blessing. We need not take up very much time
with the man himself. There is no figure more familiar upon the
pages of the Old Testament than Jacob, but let us glance at him for
a moment or two. He was a man of restless and ceaseless activity.
My own opinion is that Isaac might have done what my father did:
offered me a penny—a shekel in his case—to sit still for five minutes.
I never got that penny, and I do not think Jacob would have done.
Restless, ceaseless in his activity, but always believing in God.
There is no story in the life of Jacob but that we find his faith in
God underlying it and surrounding it; and yet he was ever attempt-

ing to help God by making his own clever arrangements. That is the story of Jacob very briefly told.

Now mark the conflicting facts. Faith desired an entry into the blessing of his father. Fear secured it by trickery. Before that, faith desired the birthright, which was his by Divine arrangement. Fear secured it by meanness, taking advantage of a hungry brother. Faith desired the land, and fear sought to gain it by astuteness. There is a conflict all through between this underlying and ever living fact of his faith, and his fear; and the fear led him to do most foolish things. That is something we have all done sometimes, attempting to help God. I know there is an old saying that God helps those who help themselves; but God help anybody who is imagining that he can, in the last analysis, help the fulfilment of Divine purpose in his life. That is the story of Jacob.

It is a remarkable story. Seven times, according to the records, God appeared to Abraham, five times He appeared to Jacob. In Abraham's case every appearance suggested some new venture of faith, and Abraham obeyed. In every case of the five appearances to Jacob God came and appeared for correction, overtaking his blunders, and setting his feet anew upon the pathway of obedience. All five appearances were corrective.

Now this is the man, astute, clever, scheming—I may as well use the word in our modern sense, not in the American sense, which has almost a complimentary meaning. He was cunning, in our sense of cunning, as in the case of his dealing with Laban. Although I am bound to say that I always thank God that he was one too many for Laban. Laban was the meanest man I find on the pages of the Old Testament, willing to squeeze everything out of a man, and then fling him away. He did not get away with it in the case of Jacob, with the cattle, and the women too. I am always thankful for that. We see all through in that relationship this man's faith mastered him, though his fear that God was going to break down made him foolish enough to try to help God.

That is a very brief sketch of the man. Now let us turn to the blessing, and observe these terms. Notice here is another illustration of the fact that the law of primogeniture is not upheld in the Biblical records. Here, for some reason we do not quite see, Manasseh was the elder, but it was not upon him that the right hand of Jacob dwelt. The left hand was put there; and the old man had to cross his hands. When Joseph had brought them in, he had arranged it so that his father's right hand should be placed upon Manasseh, and the left hand upon Ephraim. The old man crossed his hands so that the right rested upon Ephraim, and the left upon Manasseh, and when Joseph protested the old man said, I know what I am doing. Not, of course, in those 'words, but that is the effect of what he said, and undoubtedly he did know.

That is an interesting side-line of study. Follow it through, and we find Ephraim became the dominating tribe in Israel, Manasseh became a tribe sadly failing. However we are interested in the blessing that Jacob pronounced, as he pronounced it.

Notice first the difference in the blessing of Joseph and that of his sons. In Genesis xlviii it is said he blessed Joseph, and then that he blessed his sons. So this is really the blessing of Joseph through his sons. What was he doing? He was first of all reviewing his own experiences. In interpreting the blessing we must see that faith recognized God. "The God before Whom my fathers Abraham and Isaac did walk, the God which hath fed me all my life long unto this day, the Angel which hath redeemed me from all evil." The same Person is referred to all through. God is seen working through an Angel; and what Jacob says is that that Angel has redeemed him from all evil. These are synonymous references to the same Person. Jacob is reviewing the way in which God had led him. The supreme note is that of redemption from all evil.

The word "evil" there means breaking up—ruin. He says God had redeemed him from that. It was the redemption, the act of the next-of-kin who assumed responsibility. It comes from that word "Goel." The next-of-kin assumed responsibility to extricate, as a kinsman, from trouble. Said Jacob at the end of life: That is what God has been all the way through, redeeming me from all possible break-down and ruin. How often he had failed, but he was looking back, and he said: All the way God has redeemed me. God has proved my Kinsman—Redeemer, bringing me through and out of all the faults and failures of my own wrong-doing; God, the Angel Who hath redeemed me from all evil.

There we see at last the Angel Who has identified Himself with him; God has identified Himself with him, delivered him from all his wrong-doing, and their consequences, and has restored the broken harmony. That was Jacob's outlook upon life. Go back in the record to chapter xlii. There we read that when he was speaking to some of his sons who had come back from Joseph in Egypt, and they had told him that they must take Benjamin down there, because the man in government had told them that he would not see them again, and would do nothing for them unless they brought Benjamin, Jacob their father said, "Me ye have bereaved of my children; Joseph is not, and Simeon is not, and ye will take Benjamin away; *all these things are against me.*" That was the outlook then. But now, over against that, "The Angel which hath redeemed me from all evil." That is the outlook of faith. That outlook of faith made the gathering shadows shine with the bright light of faith then. Now he did not say, "All these things are against me"; but all these things have been working together, under the guidance and the goodness of God, for my good. I have been redeemed from all evil. The clear vision had come to him.

It is a great picture of this old man; a fascinating story at the end of life, with trembling hands stretched out and crossed and laid upon the heads of those two lads; reviewing his past in order that he might express his desire for Joseph and these two lads. "The God before Whom my fathers Abraham and Isaac did walk, the God Which hath fed me all my life long unto this day, the Angel which hath redeemed me from all evil, bless the lads. Let my name be named on them, and the name of my fathers Abraham and Isaac; and let them grow into a multitude in the midst of the earth." The Angel of His presence bless the lads. It was a review of the whole of life, at the end of life; and there his faith that was always present flamed out, and he corrected the mistake that he had made when he said: "All these things are against me," and declared that the Angel had redeemed him from all evil.

That is the point in the life story of Jacob upon which the writer of this letter fastens, because that was the moment when his faith became absolutely triumphant, and expressed itself most clearly. There is a great comfort in this story as it reveals to us the patience of God, honouring faith however feeble, however trembling it may be. When a man said to God, in the Person of His Son, "Lord, I believe, help mine unbelief," at once what he desired was accomplished for him. Faith was honoured. He always honours faith, however weak, however feeble, if it be the master fact of the life, if it underlie all things. God is infinitely patient, and honours it.

But it is equally true that faith makes possible the action of God. Yes, Jacob, you are quite right, the God before Whom your fathers Abraham and Isaac walked has been your God, and He has fed you all the days of your life; and the Angel of His presence has redeemed you from all evil. But the fact abides that by faith you are able at last to tell that story, and to tell it so completely; and you told it in terms of blessing upon the sons of your boy

Joseph, whom you thought you had lost when you said: "All these things are against me." You were thinking of the loss of Joseph, and thinking of the possible loss of Benjamin; and now things have turned out, not as you expected them to, because the Angel of His presence has redeemed you from all evil.

It is full of comfort, and though we may be very conscious at times of foolishness and faltering and feebleness, have we faith? Yes, we have faith, and if we have it, God will honour it, and at last in all likelihood we shall review the way along which He has taken us, and confess that faith has been the principle of our victory, and God has acted because of our faith.

XI

The Faith of Joseph

SCRIPTURE LESSON - Gen. l. 22-26; Exod. xiii. 19; Josh. xxiv. 32

"By faith Joseph, when his end was nigh, made mention of the
departure of the children of Israel; and gave commandment concerning his bones" -   -   -   -   -   Hebrews xi. 22

W E have noticed that the writer of this letter seems to dismiss
three outstanding personalities with very brief reference. I am
referring to verses 20, 21, and 22, concerning Isaac, Jacob, and
Joseph. There is no lengthy account of either of these men. The
writer in each case has fastened upon the illustration of faith that
came when they were at the end of life. In the reference to the
faith of Joseph is found the words, "By faith Joseph, when his end
was nigh." There is nothing more wonderful in this chapter, nor
more interesting, than the variety of the stories, the different circumstances in which faith is seen in operation. That becomes
even a little more remarkable when we go on beyond what we are
doing now. Here we have something different to anything we
have seen. The circumstances were different. The person in
many respects is different from his father, Jacob, and his grandfather,
Isaac, or from Abraham, of from any others to whom reference is
made by the writer. Under what varied circumstances it appears,
and how triumphant in those varied circumstances.

This statement concerning Joseph is a most remarkable one.
The story of Joseph is well known. Is there a story we have loved
more, from our childhood up? It stands out, different from all the
rest, and yet most remarkable, and I do not hesitate to use the word,
fascinating to children and young life; and equally fascinating as
the years pass, with yet a greater glory and glow. The story in its
entirety is well known, and I need not tarry now particularly with
the characteristics of this man. Again we have something entirely
different from his father and his grandfather, and from his great-
grandfather; different from any at which we have looked. If
asked to speak of the characteristics of Joseph, I wonder how I
should describe them. I think I should describe him first of all as
ingenuous, artless, but not a fool. I should describe him as fearless

in a very remarkable way as that is manifested throughout the story. Then of course he was a statesman, with all the remarkable qualities of statesmanship; and he brought them to bear upon the welfare of, the people, which also is an interesting fact, that I am not going to discuss now. We have heard a great deal during the last generation of men obtaining a corner on something. Well, that is the first corner you read about. Joseph gained a corner on wheat, but he did not do it for his own enrichment. He did it for the good of the people. That was real statesmanship.

Throughout he was actuated by faith, to which I am going to return quite briefly in conclusion. I am now primarily concerned with the manifestation of his faith, to which the writer of this letter draws attention. "By faith Joseph, when his end was nigh," when all the interesting and fascinating things recorded concerning him were coming to conclusion, and very soon he would have done with earthly affairs and pass on into the life that lies beyond, mysterious and marvellous, "when his end was nigh," what did he do? "He made mention of the departure of the children of Israel, and gave commandment concerning his bones."

Surely it is quite a remarkable declaration concerning faith. It is faith at the very end, when he speaks of his nation, and their departure; and here is the act of faith; commands something concerning his bones. The man is dying. He will soon be gone. Yes, he knows it, and he is thinking of it, that his bones will be left behind, and he has a thought concerning his bones.

Of course it has often been observed, it is noticeable that all the Genesis story, beginning in primal order and beauty, then recording disastrous failure, and all the goodness of God and stupidity of man, ends with the significant words, "a coffin in Egypt." In that coffin there were bones. They had embalmed him after the Egyptian custom; and the act of faith to which this writer refers, is what he said about those bones. He mentioned the departure of the children of Israel, and gave them instruction that when they departed, they should carry up his bones.

Let us see how faith was operating. First consider the command in itself; then consider the commandment as indicating the activity of faith; then in conclusion, as I have twice already said, I want us to see that commandment concerning his bones was consonant with all the attitudes of his life.

Now to begin with, the command in itself. What was Joseph talking about? Have in mind his position at the moment. He was talking about the departure of the children of Israel, and gave commandment that when they departed, his bones were to be carried up with them. The departure of the children of Israel. Now we must get back into the actual historic setting of this fact. We must notice where these people were, and then think of them as living where they were. Departing and going into Canaan is, in itself, a strange thing. The departure of the children of Israel was contrary to reasonableness. Why should they leave Egypt? Why should they go back into Canaan? Canaan had never been kind to them up till now. It certainly had not been kind to Joseph. You remember he reached Canaan when he was about six or seven years old, a motherless boy, and I am afraid it must be admitted, not that I think it had a great effect upon his character, I think his father rather petted him and spoiled him, that child of Rachel, his dearly loved. Canaan was not kind to him. Again, there sprang up the hostility of his brethren. Loved by his father, cared for by his father, and loyal to his father; but if you have ten or eleven brothers hostile to you, you do not have the easiest time. I do not say that of experience, but of observation. No, his memory of Canaan could not be a particularly happy one; and certainly his father and his brethren and their families had not found Canaan particularly happy. The last thing had been there was a scarcity of food, and they were driven out of Canaan by hunger, in order to obtain something to eat. It was not reasonable to talk about going back. It was faith that talked about going back, and not reason.

And yet again. It was contrary to all appearances. There was no appearance at the time when Joseph laid that commandment upon them, that they would ever go back. They were living then, we know, in most comfortable circumstances. They were occupying the land of Goshen, and it was the most fertile and beautiful part in the land of Egypt. It was an irrigated land, a plain, a land fit for flocks—and they were shepherds. Why should they leave it? Remember that this commandment of Joseph was given 144 years before the exodus. It was not then a people enslaved to whom he gave that commandment. That came later with all its brutal bitterness, but it was not true now. They were well off. They were cared for. They were in a most privileged position; and even when they were afraid, after the death of Jacob, that Joseph would turn on them and requite them, he promised he would nourish them, and he was able to keep the promise. All the conditions made it contrary to any necessity to go. Why talk about leaving, and going back to Canaan? Appearances did not suggest a journey. What did? Faith, and already you see gleaming through the story the fact that we have been looking at the natural outlook, and faith always looks beyond that; and if it does not, it is not faith at all.

What was the supernatural outlook? They were the people of God. They knew that. They knew their history. They knew the purpose of God as it had been revealed by God to the great founder, Abraham, and repeated to Isaac and Jacob, and unquestionably it was well known to Joseph himself. He knew that in the Divine purpose those people were not going to stay in Egypt. I do not for a moment say that Joseph saw what would happen. In that dark time when another Pharaoh arose that knew not Joseph, they were led into the most brutal form of slavery. But he did see beyond it, and his outlook was that they could not stay there, that there must come the day when they went back to the land, which, as he said, God had promised to Abraham, and to Isaac and Jacob.

And now the act of personal faith. He knew his relationship with that people, and he knew that he would not be there when they marched, when they actually left Egypt and went back to Canaan. Not only was he ignorant of the circumstances; he had no knowledge of when they would go, but he knew he would not be there. Carry my bones up; I belong to you, I belong to this movement; I am in this purpose of God, and though as to bodily presence, and the possibility of help and leadership I shall not be there, at any rate carry my bones up. "By faith he spake of the departure of the children of Israel, and gave commandment concerning his bones."

Now mark well the activity of faith as seen there. First of all it was the outward and onward look that made him give that commandment. He was not looking at circumstances. He knew them, he saw them, it is quite evident; but all his activities show how alive he was to the facts in the midst of which they were living, and in which he was living and exercising his authority. Faith is the assurance of things hoped for, and assurance means confidence; and in the soul of Joseph burned the confidence that one day God's purpose must be fulfilled, however unreasonable it appeared at the present moment. That is faith. Faith is the assurance, the confidence of things hoped for, and therefore he was looking not only through and on, but into the meaning of the present; and looking into the meaning of the present he knew perfectly well that the future must be according to the Divine purpose. "He made mention of the departure of the children of Israel"; faith in the purpose of God. He was proving in his soul the reality of the things not seen. He could not see anything that led to the expectation of return to Canaan. Indeed it did not seem politic to go back, or reasonable; and it certainly did not seem to be possible; but he saw the Divine purpose, and therefore he gave commandment, and he chose in his activity of faith, identification with the people of God. A statesman, I called him. Never was the greatness of his statesmanship more adequately revealed than here, when all statesmanship on the earthly level was ceasing, when he was at the end. This great statesman took in the sweep of the ages, and the Divine purpose, and said: When you march, carry my bones up.

Now finally for a moment, I want you to see that this final activity on the part of Joseph was consonant with the attitude of his life. There is nothing more arresting. Take the Bible, and go through for yourselves to see how, in all sorts of circumstances this man reckoned with God, believed in God, based his confidence upon that reckoning and upon that belief; and because he had done so, when he had got to the end, that same confidence expressed itself as he gave commandment concerning his bones.

Go over the ground with me in the quickest way possible. Do you see him in the house of Potiphar, a young man in all the flush and strength and beauty of his young manhood, faced with a terrible temptation? How did he overcome? I am quoting his words:

"How can I do this great wickedness, and sin against God?" Delivered from temptation and in the prison because he believed in God.

Follow him to the prison. He is there for a long time, gaining the respect of the prisoners and the warders, until there comes an hour when certain of those in authority come to him. They have learned enough of him to know he can help them. They asked him to explain the strange dreams, the baker and the butler. He had to wait a long time. When they asked him the meaning of their dreams do you remember what he said?

"Do not interpretations belong to God?"

There is the recognition again. He is going to interpret. Yes, but he says it belongs to God. He had to wait two whole years after the interpretations. The baker was executed, and the butler was delivered. You remember the telling little sentence, "the butler forgat Joseph." Of course that is another story. I shall never forget once hearing Thomas Champness read that chapter, and the only comment he made was when he read that verse. He said, "And his name is not always Butler!"

But then things happened. Now next we see him before Pharaoh. The butler has told his story. Joseph has been sent for, and he is standing before Pharaoh, and Pharaoh in words characterized by honour, and even flattery, sought an interpretation of these strange dreams he had had. Well, what did Joseph say?

"God shall give Pharaoh an answer of peace. . . . The thing is established by God, and God will shortly bring it to pass."

There he stood now in the presence of the great ruler, out of the prison and in the court, and he is asked for an interpretation; and he says the same thing he said to the prisoners, "It is not in me, it is in God."

Then we come to that matchless scene in which he is before his brethren, those men who had treated him so ill, those men who had nearly broken their father's heart by lying about the boy. The father thought the boy was dead, and undoubtedly the brothers did, or hoped he was. They thought it was all over. Nothing is all over when it happens. All things will get up and look at you one day, and if not on this side of the grave, then on the other. It is very valuable and important to remember that. I see him then before his brothers, and they are strangely perturbed. Naturally they were. What did he say to them? He attributed his success to God. "God hath made me fruitful in the land of my affliction."

And then, "God did send me before you to preserve life."

Even more emphatic, "It was not you who sent me hither, but God."

They had sent him. They had been responsible. No, he said, there is someone higher than you over all your machinations. God saw the famine, He knew it was coming; He sent me before you to make provision for you.

And in that hour he was the supreme ruler. All power had been given to him, and wielded by him. What did he say about that? I have become the supreme Lord in the land of Egypt. Nothing of the kind. What did he say? "God hath made me lord of all Egypt."

We see all the way, wherever we follow him; and when his father was dying, and his brethren were frightened, what did he say to them? Oh yes, I know, I know what was in your mind. I know that you wanted to kill me, or get rid of me.

"Ye meant evil against me, but God meant it for good."

What a triumph, a man who could see through the immediate to the ultimate, a man who could see beyond all the machinations of men the purpose and the power of Almighty God. That is Joseph, and that is the man who at the end said, "I die." Yes, he knew. He knew the end was close at hand.

"But God will surely visit you, and bring you up out of this land, unto the land which He sware to Abraham, to Isaac, and to Jacob." I die. God has made me ruler over all Egypt for the time being, and He has sent me to get ready for you. You meant evil. But there is something higher, and that is God; and God meant it for good, overruling even your folly and your sin in the interest of humanity. God meant it for good.

And then what lies behind all this? God will bring you up out of this land. You are not going to stay here. This is not the appointed place for you. Canaan is the place. How do you know, Joseph? God sware it to Abraham, unto Isaac and to Jacob; and because God has arranged it, no circumstances can change it. God will visit you. You will leave Egypt. You will go up to that land. I will be dead; carry my bones out. At any rate associate me so far in the covenant and purpose of God. It was great faith, the faith of a life triumphing, when life was ending, and when all the larger movements from which he would be excluded on the earth level in the government of God would come to fulfilment; at any rate, take my bones up with you.

It is a glorious picture, not a forlorn and battered soul trusting in God; but blessed be His holy name, the picture of a great and successful man, seeing that the greatest things were yet to come; and desiring to express his confidence in those things, and his desire in some measure to be identified with the movement. Yes, a great and successful man, seeing that the greatest things were yet to come, and sure of them because he was sure of God.

I prefer to leave the study at that point, believing that we shall see faith now acting perhaps as we have not seen it at all in this chapter before; acting in the case of a man such as Joseph was, who had risen to such a position of power; and had provided for his family in a wonderful and generous way through Pharaoh's agreement; and seeing the interval, but seeing beyond all intervals to the purpose of God, and saying, I die; you will go; carry my bones up; and let that be the sacramental symbol of my relationship with the Divine movement.

XII

The Faith of Amram and Jochebed

Scripture Lesson - - - - - Exodus ii. 1-10

"By faith Moses, when he was born, was hid three months by his parents, because they saw he was a goodly child; and they were not afraid of the king's commandment" - Hebrews xi. 23

No, this is not the story of faith on the part of Moses. As the text is read casually and a little superficially, the first words might deflect our thought, and we hurry on, getting to the next verse: "By faith, Moses." But there is nothing about Moses' faith in this verse. The only action of his on record proves he had no faith. The only thing we are told about him is that the baby cried. I am not surprised. When those dear little eyes looked up into a strange woman's face he was frightened. I well remember when my youngest boy was born, I did not see him for three months. I was three months away on the other side of the continent, in America. When I came home, of course I took him in my arms, and he nearly yelled the house down! It was natural too. That is all you know about Moses here, although it was not faith, there was no blame attached to him. When the lid was lifted, and Pharaoh's daughter opened the receptacle, the baby wept. Imagine the baby of a Hebrew mother who had grown to love the face of his mother, and Miriam, his sister, looking up and seeing a strange Egyptian woman looking at him. Of course he cried. That is all there is in the story about Moses. This had nothing to do with his faith. The faith referred to here is that of his parents, and that is our theme. "By faith Moses, when he was born, was hid three months by his parents, because they saw he was a goodly child; and they were not afraid of the king's commandment."

The narrative in itself which I read, only speaks of the action of his mother; but the writer of the letter to the Hebrews, I have no doubt inspired, and fully acquainted with the facts, said "parents." His father had part in the business. I think the father had a share in the preparations. I can imagine the father preparing that little cradle of papyrus, daubing it with bitumen, and getting it ready.

At any rate the writer of the letter to the Hebrews says "his parents."

Now who were they? I do not know whether other preachers feel as I do. I am tempted now to be tremendously rude. I may be all wrong, but I do not believe one out of a hundred could tell me the names of his parents. I am talking of the great generality, and yet the names are distinctly given. His father's name was Amram, and his mother's name was Jochebed. You will find his father is mentioned fourteen times in genealogical tables and in no other way. Twice he is referred to as the husband of Jochebed. Four times he is referred to as the father of Moses and Aaron. Jochebed is only mentioned twice, both times as the wife of Amram, once as the mother of Moses and Aaron; once as the mother of Moses, Aaron, and Miriam.

Amram and Jochebed, two of the crowd, yet the very fact we do not remember their names is a very interesting and very significant one. Who were they? Two of the common crowd of slaves, not outstanding personalities. They were just two, son and daughter by succession, of Levi, and they had joined their lives together, but they were in slavery. Think with me for a moment, and only a moment, of the conditions then existing. Moses was born 64 years after the death of Joseph. A great deal can happen in 64 years, and as we know, a great deal of tragic happenings had taken place in that period; as the writer of the book of Exodus tells us in his first chapter, another Pharaoh had arisen that knew not Joseph. It is quite evident that he resented the presence of these people in the land of Goshen, and their great success, and their rapid multiplication. The result was the whole of them had become reduced to slavery, and it was a brutal slavery, too. There came a time when they had to make bricks without straw. Think of that when you next look at the pyramids. They were built at that time, and by those people. As I hurry over this, I want you to notice they were enslaved, and still multiplying so rapidly that Pharaoh adopted a new policy. He had determined to prevent the growth of the people by killing every boy born. That was the edict of the king. There had been an interesting event in the case of the Egyptian midwives, who refused to carry out the king's command. Since they would not do it, it became a national order; when a boy was born, the king's order was he should be flung into the Nile, and drowned. Those were the conditions. This baby was born under those conditions. It is just a beautiful human story if read in that way all through; and seeing he was a goodly child, his parents hid him for three months, and when the baby's crying was louder than it was at the beginning, when it was impossible to hide the fact that the baby was there—I do not know where they hid him for three months—but when they could no longer hide him, they then took action.

What was the action? They committed him to the river of death. They put him in that ark of bulrushes, or papyrus, covered him over, and took the little precious ark, with the child in it, and put him down in the flags or reeds growing there, and sent his sister to watch what would happen.

Well you know the issue, and here is seen the sublimity of faith in its simplest manifestation, and that is the thing that obsesses me, that possesses me, as I follow this history of the triumphs of faith. These two unknown, hidden people, two of the slave crowd! Now when the writer of the letter to the Hebrews says that their action was one of faith, you have a revelation that does not appear in Exodus. We can read the Exodus story and imagine their action was one of pure love and affection for the baby. I have little doubt it was that; but now I have found out something else. These two people of the oppressed race, in slavery, believed in God. "He that cometh to God must believe that He is." They believed somehow He was an over-ruling God. He that cometh to God must not only believe that he is, but that "He is a Rewarder of those who diligently seek Him." I am quoting from the context, as you know. And there when they made that ark, and when they put the baby therein, and when they placed him on the river of death in the flags, and watched, it was an act of faith. Simple folk, but very sublime faith.

I want to name four elements in the faith of those two people. First of all it was faith inspiring hope. Secondly, it was faith creating courage. Thirdly it was faith acting rationally. Finally it was faith, all unconsciously co-operating with the purpose of God. This was not Abel, Enoch, Abraham; it was not Isaac, Jacob, Joseph, those great towering figures. Just two slaves, two of the common crowd, but what they did, they did by faith. I want very briefly to take those four things, asking you to look at them.

First it was faith inspired by hope. Of course, there was a sense of love and affection. They saw he was a goodly child, but they knew the utter hopelessness of circumstances. Whenever a boy was born, he was being slain, flung into the waters of the Nile; but these two people knew this, that in spite of all apparent hopelessness, God remained. I am not suggesting that they knew what would happen. The text shows they did not know at all, but their action was a venture made upon God, and in their souls, the souls

of father and mother, those parents, there was a hope, and they had
faith in God that inspired hope, the hope that the little life might
be spared. It was a great and venturesome faith in the presence of
apparently the most hopeless circumstances.

Again it was faith creating courage. Notice what the writer
says: "They were not afraid of the king's commandment." Now
of course that is ultimate finding, and it is true. There is a sense
in which they knew the danger of the king's commandment, and
that if they did not cast the baby into the river, if the word reached
the king or court, the boy would be cast in; and what they did they
did in spite of the king, in spite of the king's commandment. In
other words, they were convinced that there was an authority and
power higher than that of Pharaoh. Pharaoh said, Kill these boys.
These two said: We will not kill this boy. In faith we are thinking
and believing in a higher Power and Authority.

Then the story is very interesting because I see here faith acting
rationally. You say, what do you mean by that? Look at that
ark of bulrushes. It was an act of reason, carefully prepared. Look
at that girl, the sister, sent to watch what would happen. It was a
rational activity, and yet mark the ready wit, whether the ready
wit of Miriam or the mother's instruction. When the daughter of
Pharaoh came and lifted the lid, and the baby cried, Miriam at
once said: "Shall I find thee a nurse?" Faith is never foolhardy.
Faith is always rational. Faith believes in God, and does the thing
that appeals to the reason. Some of you are expecting I will quote
something. I will not disappoint you. It was a profound word
Cromwell used: "Trust in God, and keep your powder dry."
I think England needs to hear that again. I am not apologising for
saying that. They prepared the ark, they put the baby in it, closed
the lid, and by the river of death they laid it, if perchance, something might transpire, and they put Miriam to watch; and when the
thing happened that must have surprised Miriam, she with ready
wit—I shall always think her own wit rather than her mother's
instruction, because Jochebed would not have an idea it would
happen—she saw something kindling in the eyes of that Egyptian
woman, some smile passing over her face; and she said: Shall I
fetch a nurse for the child; and that rational action was at once
responded to. The daughter of Pharaoh said, "Go," and she went,
and she found Jochebed, and she took the child and nursed it.

We are told that when the child grew she took him to Pharaoh's
daughter, and he became her son. I wonder if anyone has sure
information—I have not; if so, I shall be glad to have it. I can

speculate with any man born—but I wonder how long Jochebed had him before she handed him over to Pharaoh's daughter. There are old expositors who believe she had full charge of him until he was twelve. It is far more likely she was in the palace to which she, a slave woman, would be admitted, the nurse of the adopted boy of Pharaoh's daughter. You read in the Bible of a child being weaned. Of course, this is going away back to the very beginnings of Hebrew history. Do you know when it was a child was weaned? Weaning did not mean what it does now to some of you to-day. The age at which the child was said to be weaned, when it ceased to be a helpless infant and become a child clinging to his mother's apron strings, was twelve years. Now I am doing a little speculating with the rest in believing Jochebed had charge of Moses until he was twelve at the court, under the watchful eyes of Pharaoh's daughter, and surrounded by court attendants; but I think his mother watched over him. I think in those years she told him stories of Abraham, of Isaac, of Jacob, of Joseph, that wonderful leader, through whom the people had gone down into Egypt before the new Pharaoh arose. I think she stored the mind of the boy with the history of her people. We are taking next the story of Moses himself. How did he know he was a member of that race? What inspired him to take the part of a member of that race and get himself into trouble? What made him try to mediate between two members of the race? I think he knew his history. You have the baby committed by faith to the care of the mother.

Very well, faith inspiring hope, faith creating courage and rational thinking; and now the greatest thing of all, something Jochebed did not know, something Amram was unconscious of. What were they doing? Faith unconsciously was co-operating with God. What was the human issue of this act? The cry of the baby admitted him to the heart of a woman. That woman admitted him to the court of Pharaoh. She adopted him, and moreover, educated him, for Stephen in his great Apologia says in the Acts: "Moses was instructed in all the wisdom of the Egyptians; and he was mighty in his words and works." That was not a reference to what happened later on, but in all those years. That is the issue, but that is the human level, but it is a wonderful issue.

But look again. What did they do when they put that child in the ark, and committed it in faith, a faith that groped, and did not actually know; certainly did not know how the thing was going to turn out, but a faith that was certain of God, and made a great venture upon that consciousness? What were they doing?

They were finding and preserving the life of a man, and such a man. No, I am not going to follow that any longer save to say this. If you want to know how great he was, well listen to this from the last chapter of Exodus:

"The Lord spake unto Moses face to face as a man speaketh unto his friend."

That is the baby that they saved.

Or turn over to Deuteronomy, its closing chapter, and in that chapter, added by some other hand after his passing, what does he say?

"Moses whom the Lord knew face to face."

Amram and Jochebed did not foresee this thing; but they believed God, they believed in God. They did not know what was going to happen, or what would take place. They did not know what the issue would be; but believing, by faith they prepared the ark. They put the baby in it; they committed it to the waters of death, and then waited, and that was the issue.

There is no need for me to hold this congregation at any length to drive home the lesson. Let me state it in briefest words. The principle of faith operating, works mightier issues than it knows. Is your principle of faith operating in the case of your children? You will not be here: will have crossed over long before the issue. What will be the result of your training? Many years ago there was a brilliant writer in her young days. She married, and after a number of years she went to see an old college friend, who said to her: "My dear, we have had no books from you for many years. I think it is a pity you gave up writing books." To which she replied to her friend: "I have not given up writing books. I have written two." "What are their titles?" she asked. "'Ethel' and 'Albert,' those are my children." "Your children!" "Yes, and I am trying to write living epistles known and read of all men that they have been with Jesus." No, you cannot put the measurements on the issue of your act of faith upon the immediate. I repeat therefore, the principle of faith operating, works mightier issues than it knows.

And the other thing is that this principle of faith is possible to the lowliest slaves, and may act in apparently trivial matters, and yet it may be the way of bringing about the higher things which are the highest and the sublimest of them all. Let us thank God that in this marvellous chapter chronicling the triumphs of faith the writer was led, as I believe of the Spirit, to include this action of two people, little known, hidden away among the crowds of

6

slaves; and so much so that even to this day very few people really know their names; and yet they by an act of venturesome superlative faith marched with God, and created vantage ground upon which He marched forward in the fulfilment of His high purpose.

XIII

The Faith of Moses

SCRIPTURE LESSON - - - - Hebrews xi. 24-28
"By faith Moses refused to be called the son of Pharaoh's
daughter" - - - - - - Hebrews xi. 24
"By faith he forsook Egypt" - - - Hebrews xi. 27
"By faith he kept the Passover" - - Hebrews xi. 28

IN our last study we were considering the previous verse in this chapter: "By faith Moses, when he was born, was hid three months by his parents, because they saw he was a goodly child; and they were not afraid of the king's commandment." It is well to remember that what we have read as a lesson is the record of the activity of faith also, and an activity of faith resulting from the faith of Amram and Jochebed. All the story of Moses is rooted in the faith of Amram and Jochebed, just two unknown people of the common vulgar slave crowd. They exercised faith when they committed the baby to the river of death. Now all we have read is the result.

The close connection between the story of Moses and the story of his parents is one that we should bear in mind. This, then, is the record of the activity of faith in the case of a man of whom I am inclined to say Dr. Kyle was justified when he said of Moses: "The greatest man among mere men in the whole history of the world." I quite think that is a justified conclusion. Once more, and then I expect to dismiss it, whatever is here about Moses is the result of the faith of his father and mother.

We are all familiar with the wonderful story of the life of Moses lasting 120 years, and those years clearly divided into three forties. Just recall the facts as I give you not sentences, but phrases. Forty years in the court as prince. Forty years in the wilderness as shepherd. Forty years in the wilderness as leader of a nation.

Now the writer of this letter describes the faith of this man. As I am pondering it through the days I get more and more amazed. I am amazed at something for our next study, and more amazed still at something that follows that. But the amazing thing, in dealing with Moses, is that the writer has taken the illustrations of his faith from two points of crisis in his life; one, his departure from the court, and two, illustrating the faith of a nation: and there he says two things about that. There is nothing said about his faith in the first forty years, not that he was without it. All his subsequent actions prove that his faith in God was living long before this great choice was made, and indeed, operated in the making of the choice. But this writer does not refer to anything of the past, but he tells that by faith he refused, by faith he forsook, by faith he kept—may I change my word? Some expositors do not agree with the change, "by faith he *instituted* the Passover." Two great crises in his life, illustrating the activity of his faith.

Therefore we have three things to look at. First of all the great renunciation made by faith. Secondly, the fact of the Exodus as the result of faith; and thirdly, the method of that fact, the institution and observance of the Passover.

The first of these, of course, is in some senses the most arresting, because the writer is singularly careful to tell us exactly what happened, and I am going to read not merely my first verse as a text, but a little more.

"By faith Moses, when he was grown up, refused to be called the son of Pharaoh's daughter, choosing rather to be evil entreated with the people of God, than to enjoy the pleasures of sin for a season; accounting the reproach of Christ greater riches than the treasures of Egypt."

Let us watch the mental process, because that is what this writer has done. He has revealed a mental process, and the final fact is first stated—"he refused." But on what basis did he refuse? "Choosing." How did he come to choose? "Accounting." The psychology of the thing is all there. The writer is watching these things, and gathering up into clear, sharp, crystal sentences the account of the process through which Moses passed. How long the process took we do not know, but we have the three things. The final, the ultimate thing is, he "refused." That which preceded the refusal was the choice—"choosing." And the choice was made as the result of another process, perhaps longer than either of them, because the final would be immediate, complete. He refused, and the choosing would not take long. It was deliberate, but there was something preceding it—"accounting." We see the mind process.

Suppose we take that mind process in the other order from which the writer of the letter to the Hebrews has given it to us, and try and see what was happening in the case of Moses. "Accounting," and the word merely means balancing things, in order to come to a decision of some sort, putting this by the side of that, and weighing the evidence on both sides: "accounting." He may have been a long time doing that. He left Egypt when he was forty, and you see some evidence of what he had been thinking in the story you find in the Old Testament. But here the writer sums it all up, "accounting." He had been looking at things, looking at Egypt, looking at these people who were by this time in slavery, amongst them his own father and mother, the mother who had nursed him; and he had been accounting.

Well, what did he see? Two things. First, I am not putting them in the order of statement, but backwards; first "the treasures of Egypt." I am not going to indulge in any description of what those treasures were. Suffice it to say we know well, and better than our fathers did, how marvellous were the treasures of Egypt. They had a remarkable civilization. They had untold wealth. The splendour of its court was magnificent. The treasures in Egypt. He looked at it all, the wealth and the power—listen—of the oppressors. Egypt was oppressing the Hebrew people with great cruelty, for there had arisen another Pharaoh, and from that time things turned out hardly for them, and now they were being treated with brutal cruelty as the boys born were flung into the Nile, except this boy. This boy was saved. There may have been others; I do not know. But this boy was saved, and Moses, in this court of splendour, learning, and refinement, looked round, and saw the wealth and power.

Then he looked at the other side, and he saw the oppressed, these people, bowing the neck, under the yoke of abject slavery and poverty, which had become absolutely brutal in every way. He saw these people, the oppressed, as over against the oppressors on the one side, the oppressors with great wealth and power.

Well, what about these people? Great poverty and no power. No, that is not all he saw. He saw the reproach of the Messiah— I have resolutely changed the word from its Greek form Christ, not that it is inaccurate, to the Hebrew form, Messiah. He found these enslaved people had a hope of a Messiah, of a Deliverer; and in spite of all the oppression, and in spite of all the brutality, that hope was still there, and that hope was bringing all of them into a place of even deeper reproach. Not merely the brutality of the slave-masters, but the ribald laughter of them at these stupid people indulging and cherishing, and living upon a hope; the reproach of it. How they laughed at them. And Moses looked at it all, accounting, accounting, putting one against the other, thinking things through; and coming to a decision on the basis of his accounting that the reproach of the Messiah among the oppressed people was greater than all the riches and power of Egypt; and on this basis he refused.

Yes, but before the definite refusal which broke with Egypt, on the basis of the accounting, there was a choosing. Follow the process through. Accounting, accounting, watching, thinking, pondering, accounting all the wealth, all the power of the oppressing Egypt; all the poverty and all the weakness, and yet this undimmed and undying hope burning in their hearts, of a Messiah.

Accounting, and there came a moment when, on the basis of this accounting, he came to a decision—choosing, choosing, literally, taking for himself a definite decision and position; balancing the long issues towards which that hope was pointing with the present affliction under which they were suffering; balancing between those two, and coming to the conclusion that he had rather, and indeed would, definitely choose to share the affliction resulting from such a hope, than enjoy the pleasures of sin for a season.

I love that passage because it is so true to life, "pleasures of sin." There are such to-day. What a stupid thing it is that some people say that there is no pleasure in sin. Of course there are pleasures in sin. Dr. Gordon, of Boston, wrote a hymn, "My Jesus, I love Thee." In many books one of the verses reads:

> "My Jesus, I love Thee, I know Thou art mine,
> For Thee all the follies of sin I resign."

I wonder what made some good dear pious soul alter that. Dr Gordon did not write that. He wrote:

> "For Thee all the pleasures of sin I resign."

I say some pious soul. There are such about. Someone thought that it would be wrong to sing about the pleasures of sin. But the writer of this letter knew. Oh, Moses saw, saw the pleasures, the pleasures of sin, saw them all in Egypt; but did you notice the little qualifying phrase, "for a season"? We can write that phrase over all the pleasures of sin that are luring us to-day. Yes, they are there, "pleasures of sin *for a season*"; and then midnight darkness and despair.

So Moses chose. He made his choice, and he made a definite decision to share with the people suffering affliction, the joy of the long result, burning within them the hope of a Messiah, rather than to take all that Egypt could offer in the way of pleasure, with its limitation, "for a season." So the action in the mind, accounting.

It may have taken a good while. Choosing, that did not take long, at least it was definite; but by faith, having in view the recompense of the reward he chose.

What was the issue, the ultimate? He refused. "He refused to be called the son of Pharaoh's daughter." He refused all the possibilities created for him on the level of the world, and the power under which he had been nurtured for forty years in the goodness of the heart of a woman. But he saw through it all. He saw clearly that it was fading, that it was for a season, that it was doomed; and he saw the hope of the Messiah bringing reproach, men laughing at it; and yet burning like a beacon; and he said: No, I will not be called the son of Pharaoh's daughter. In other words, to go back to our early consideration and the definition of faith, that was confidence in things hoped for, and conviction of things unseen, and so by faith he refused.

Then we take the next. By faith he forsook. He carried out the decision of his faith actually. Now commentators are not quite agreed as to what the writer was referring at this point when he said: "By faith he forsook Egypt, not fearing the wrath of the king." They say it was the hour when he first left Egypt, after he had killed the Egyptian, and then tried to deliver his compatriots who would not be delivered; and he went into the desert. Some say it refers to that. Others say it refers to the Exodus itself when he and the people forsook Egypt. So far as I am concerned I think it includes both. I think the statement refers to his first leaving, and forty years afterwards.

Why did he leave at first? There we are face to face with the revelation of the underlying thought of Moses. He went out, and saw an Egyptian brutally treating a Hebrew. Well, why interfere with them? Why take any notice of it? It was a commonplace matter. It was going on everywhere. Yet when he came across a concrete instance, he took the side of the Hebrew. Why did he? Why not let the Egyptian bruise him and ill-treat him? He belonged to the court. Why did he not let things go on? Can you not imagine it; the stories Jochebed had told him in those baby years had taken root in his life: Abraham, Isaac, Jacob, Joseph, then the gap; but he heard about them all, and he knew that these oppressed people had got this strange hope of a Messiah. The reproach of Him was upon them, and he stood for these people. He of the court, stood for them, a revelation of his faith. He was unable to do what he wanted to do. His heart dictated that he should do something to help his people, but quite evidently he stirred up trouble. When he found two of his brethren quarrelling and he tried to mediate between them, they said: What is it to do with you? Who made you a prince and judge? Are you going to do with us what you did to the Egyptian yesterday? So it was known, and he fled. He need not have gone. He could quite easily as a member of the court, the son of Pharaoh's daughter, make a statement which would cause him to be delivered from all trouble. But no. He was face to face with his own disability, and yet he was afraid of the wrath of the Pharaoh if it was found out, and his first flight was in fear, but it was also in faith.

Then followed forty years, to me always a very fascinating story for thought and meditation. I hope there never creeps into your thought or accent pity for Moses, that he had to give up the splendour of the court and spend forty years as a nomad, taking care of sheep under the shadow of the mountains and in the wilderness. I hope you do not pity him. It was a great life. It was a life of discipline and meditation. It was a life of training, all unknown to him, a method of preparation for what in the economy and purpose of God lay before him. No, do not pity him. Believe me, there is far more splendour and majesty under the mountains of God, and in the wilderness, which speaks of His power, than in all the courts of kings. Forty years.

And then the surprising morning, when about his ordinary calling he saw a bush burning, flaming, blazing, and drew near; and wonder of wonders, the bush burned with fire but it was not being destroyed. The lambent flames around it played, and it flourished unconsumed in fire. The call came to him, the call of God, to become the leader of the people, still oppressed, and more cruelly oppressed than ever in the land of Egypt, to be the one who should lead them out. I thank God for all these stories. The hesitation of Moses is fear, "Who am I?" and the answer of God, full of gentle satire, "Who made thy mouth?" The words I speak thou shalt speak—and so that communion with God.

After the hesitations had all ended as the result of that communion, he went down, and again you know the story. I need not tell it. He gathered the people. He led them out. He forsook Egypt, taking with him all those oppressed people into the wilderness. What was the secret? He tells you. "He endured, as seeing Him Who is invisible." Oh, the glorious paradoxes and contradictions of the life of faith. There is not a scientist in London, in England, or in the world, as a mere statement who will not smile at it, "seeing the invisible." But the humblest child of God, youth, maiden, old man or woman, those in the hey-day of life but know that he saw God. He had seen Him in the burning bush. He had held communion and had interpreted lessons of revelation as he had moved through the wilderness with his sheep. He saw God, and now he is not afraid. Fear has been banished because he has had the vision of God, and so came the great exodus.

Then the last phrase, which to me is very significant. By faith he kept, and the marginal reading of the Revised Version is "instituted." I repeat, some expositors object to it, and yet I think it is a true interpretation of the Hebrew word. He instituted the Passover, he kept it. Yes, he did; but it was an institution, and a very arresting and remarkable one. There, undoubtedly, the reference was to the keeping of the Passover in Egypt, and that was an act of obedient faith. The command had gone out from him to all these people for the taking of the lamb. Look at Moses uttering the command. Look at the people. They did what they were told, and the institution of the Passover was an act of faith. It was instituted and observed before they were delivered. It was an act of faith, and yet it became a perpetual thing. I quote from Moses who said: "It is a night to be much observed unto the Lord, to be much observed of all the children of Israel throughout their generations." By faith he instituted that Passover feast which was to be through all their history the symbol of the fundamental fact in that history, that they were a people redeemed, ransomed, released from bondage. Everything was rooted there. All those of you who love your Bibles watch it as you read your prophets and psalms and history—the perpetual reference to the fact that their whole history was rooted in that fact of redemption. By faith he instituted that feast as a perpetual symbol: by faith.

In contemplating the wonders of this man's faith let us never lose sight—forgive me for repeating it—of Amram and Jochebed. We do not know what we are doing when by faith we are dealing with our children. We may not have to commit our children to some ark of bulrushes; but we want to do something for them in a world like this, and do not look on it as unimportant. We do not know what is coming out of it.

As we take the whole story and have this wonderful recognition of faith we see a man exercising faith, who knew what it was to hesitate, knew what it was to tremble, knew what it was to make mistakes. I am taking the history without dealing with the details. As a matter of fact, at the end he was excluded from the land towards which he had been looking for forty years of wandering in the wilderness. He was excluded. And if you ask why he was excluded, one of the psalms answers you. I confess it is an amazing statement. It is one that gives one pause. The Psalmist says he was excluded because "he spake unadvisedly with his lips." We know when he did that, when he went to the people, after God had commissioned him to give them water, he was angry. He said: Must I bring water out of this rock? and he smote the rock. He spoke unadvisedly with his lips. He obeyed God, but he misrepresented the nature, the character, the spirit of God. And because of that he was excluded from the promised land.

Is that all? No. We will find the sequel in the New Testament. There came a time when Moses and Elijah stood with Jesus on the mount of transfigured glory and talked with Him about His exodos, the exodus, that is the word, the Greek word, the *exodos*, which is merely another form of our word exodus, that He was about to accomplish. Do not read merely the death He was to die. It was the breaking of bonds, the loosening of the prisoners, a marching of ransomed souls; and Jesus was going to the Cross to accomplish it. And Moses came there with Elijah, the law-giver and the reformer; and they talked together. Moses stood

> ". . . With glory wrapped around
>   On the hills he never trod;
>   And spoke of the strife that won our life
>   With the incarnate Son of God."

And so faith had its ultimate reward and vindication, long, long after, for in the economy of God things are not measured by the almanacs of this earth; and time cycles and centuries run their course; and some day out yonder and beyond, the full meaning of our act and life of faith will become evident, as in the case of Moses.

XIV

The Faith of Israel

SCRIPTURE LESSON Exodus xiv. 19-25, 30, 31; Joshua vi. 12-16, 20

"By faith they passed through the Red Sea as by dry land; which the Egyptians assaying to do were swallowed up. By faith the walls of Jericho fell down, after they had been compassed about for seven days"
Hebrews xi. 29, 3

THERE is an old and somewhat trite commonplace saying that confession is good for the soul. I am not discussing it, but I am proposing to avail myself of its suggestion, and begin my lecture to-day with a confession. The confession is that if I had had my own way, I would not have taken these two texts. And in connection with that confession, I indulge in a few moments in the form of an excursus on prejudice.

What is prejudice? It is almost invariably used in the sense that reveals it as something unworthy. Well, I certainly think that in many cases that use is justifiable. It is justifiable when prejudice becomes the inspiration of action. Then it is always unworthy. But what is prejudice after all? Prejudice is judgment beforehand, very often before full examination, very often before all the facts are known. It is judging a matter and deciding about a matter beforehand: that is prejudice.

Now prejudice may be correct, it may be right. My judgment beforehand may prove to be correct. It is a conviction. I am sorely tempted to use a word. English people must forgive it. I learned it on the other side of the water—it is a "hunch." Did you ever hear of it over here? It is a hunch. It is a great word after all, it is very forceful. Prejudice is a hunch, a presentiment if you like, and it is often right, but it is certainly often wrong. The judgment formed beforehand may be entirely mistaken for very many reasons, and this at least is to be remembered—I hinted at it already in passing, I state it and leave it—prejudice is never right when it is the basis of action. I can have my judgment beforehand, and I may be proved in the running of the years I was quite right. I have my prejudice about war just now. I may be wrong; but I

91

should be perfectly wrong if I allowed my prejudice to be the inspiration of my actions. That is all about that.

Why did I want to omit the text? Because I had a prejudice against the people. I do not mean in a wrong sense, but it seemed to me, as I have been pondering this remarkable chapter, that it is a striking thing, in the midst of all these wonderful stories about faith, that the writer should include these people at all, that he should refer to them as people of faith; and in view of their history I had that prejudice. I admit at once it is wrong. I have no right to have the prejudice, so I have made a confession, and I think my soul is helped.

Yet I said to myself, I dare not miss these verses out. They are in this record, and as I believe it is an inspired record, the summary of great truths concerning the principle and the victories of faith by an inspired pen, who am I that I should object to consider any part of the history. I have taken these texts, and any prejudice of that kind there may have been in my mind in this particular application is due, of course, to the history of these people. That sentence is enough to call to your mind the history. It is all here in the Old Testament. I am not referring to any subsequent history. I am referring to the history that began with the call of Abraham, and culminated with the crucifying of Jesus. You will remember what our Lord said about these people, and it is at least an arresting fact Matthew, Mark, and Luke all record this estimate of them which fell from the lips of our Lord. What did He call them? "A faithless and perverse generation." Well, if there is prejudice, that has been the reason of it. And yet, remember this, that one great danger threatening prejudice is that it sees failure, and is apt to forget victory.

Now the writer of this letter fell into no such error. He knew the failure of these people, and it is very significant, this is the only reference he makes to the nation, as the nation, in the matter of faith. There is no other reference to them. Oh, yes, to individuals constituting a part of the nation. The cases we have been taking illustrate that; and the massing of a great number of them, which we shall glance at presently. But the nation itself, this is the only reference to faith, and the reference is here to the nation.

I was greatly interested to notice in this twenty-ninth verse of chapter eleven, "By faith they passed through the Red Sea," that remarkable commentator and delightful expositor, Canon Farrar, has one little note against that verse, only one, and this is it: "'They'—of course that means Moses and the children of

Israel." I always think he did not like the verse to pass without reference to Moses, and he was perfectly right. The "they" certainly refers to Moses and the people. Undoubtedly he is correct, but Moses is not named, neither is Joshua named in the next verse. It is the people that were in view; and the writer of the letter to the Hebrews looking back says, "By faith they passed through the Red Sea as on dry land . . . by faith the walls of Jericho fell down." In view of such history, these declarations concerning the activity of faith on behalf of these people constitute a lurid light of warning, for they began in faith; even though the last finding concerning them, a finding proceeding from the lips of Him Who was essential Truth, and could make no mistake either, was that they were faithless, "a faithless and perverse generation."

So let us take the writer's outlook. He looks back to the beginnings of their history. He records two incidents connected with the earliest movement of these people towards nationality, and the two incidents are forty years apart. They were both, in the history of the people, hours of crisis, the crisis created for them when they left Egypt, and the crisis created for them when they actually crossed the Jordan and were entering the land. Looking back at these early incidents he sees faith operating. All we have to do is to examine the two incidents, the exodus and the taking of Jericho.

Now look back to that historic account. I need not dwell upon it. It is so familiar a story. Look at the people. Think of the people as they were at that time. They were an enslaved people and I think we may safely say that in many senses there had come to them that which always comes to an enslaved people, they had become vulgarized by their slavery. Very few of those people, if any, would remember Joseph. At the time of the exodus he had been dead 144 years; and yet, in spite of all the experiences through which they had passed of brutal treatment and enslavement of the very worst kind, they still believed in God. We see one flaming illustration of it in the case of Amram and Jochebed when they took that child and committed it to the waters of death. They believed in God. There might have been other illustrations that might be quoted. Take the illustration of Joshua. Joshua was born in slavery, and lived unquestionably for forty years in Egypt under these terrible conditions; and then he came out, and at once was seen at the right hand of Moses, his helper. They believed in God. I think we are justified in saying that their belief in God persisted, but as to His government, and the method of His government they were largely ignorant. They were uninstructed. They had not received the Law. They had not received the revelation of God that had been given to them through the Law and the sacred ritual. I am only trying to remember the condition of these people.

Now while they were in that condition there suddenly arrived in their midst, Moses. There were those who would remember that he had left the country forty years before. Undoubtedly they had often seen him in costly apparel, the son of Pharaoh's daughter, the heir-apparent to the throne in all probability; possibly they had seen him, knowing him to be of their race, moving among the courtly splendours of Egypt, and he had disappeared. I have no doubt the story had gone all round how he had delivered an Israelite from the brutal Egyptian, and had killed the Egyptian; and the next day sought to deliver two of his race from each other, and they had said, "Who made thee a prince and a judge over us? thinkest thou to kill me, as thou killedst the Egyptian?" and he had fled, and he had been away for forty years. They had lost sight of him, and forty years is a long time. They knew very little about him. But he came back, and what did he do? He called together the elders of Israel, and there is a gleam of light showing, that these people in all their downtrodden condition, had not broken from relationship to each other by race. They had their elders, and he called together the elders, and he told them the strange, and one would almost say the unbelievable, news that he was sent by God to lead them out of Egypt. He had called the elders and told them the news.

Do you remember what they did? It is distinctly told you. They bowed and worshipped. That bowing of the elders in the midst of a brutal slavery when called together and told that their God in Whom they had always believed, and never lost conviction concerning, that He was going to deliver them, they bowed and worshipped.

Then the activity of faith is manifest not only on the part of the elders, but on the part of the people. It is a marvellous story read with naturalness. They were told to secure a lamb and observe a feast of which they had never heard. It was to be called the feast of Passover, the feast of escape, the feast of deliverance. They were still there, bound, but they were to observe this feast, and by the hopefulness of faith they obeyed. By faith they observed the Passover. Just as we say, By faith Moses instituted the Passover, it is equally true that by faith the people observed the Passover.

Then let us thank God for these Bible stories. They hide nothing. We see the failure. We see it almost immediately. They march away out of Egypt. What a march it was, a march of faith. All the cohorts of Egypt behind them, equal to overcoming them in conflict; but they marched. There was a shadow of appalling agony over Egypt on account of the death of the first-born from the palace of Pharaoh down to the lowest cot. But they marched, and marched in faith.

Then we have the account of their march, not in a straight course, but round about. How often God leads us round about when we have to learn something, and He led them until they came to Pi-hahiroth, and there in front of them was the sea. They had come to the land's last limit. On the one side the rocky fastnesses which they could not climb; on the other Pi-hahiroth, the marshy land they could not tramp across. Only one road for them they could march. What is that? The only way was the way back. They found themselves hemmed in. That is what I meant when I said the Bible hides nothing. They complained. They grumbled. The Bible is so modern. If I may use other language, they said to Moses: We told you so. I have heard that. Haven't you? Now see what has happened. Here we are, hemmed in. We came in faith, and yet we wondered as we came. Our faith was unmixed and wondering, but here we are, hemmed in.

Then the wonderful story. Moses, great man of God, said to them: "Stand still, and see the salvation of the Lord." It was great advice, but it was a mistake. Mistake? Oh no, not in some senses. It was good; but notice what comes immediately after. It says immediately afterwards: "Wherefore criest thou unto Me? speak unto the children of Israel, that they go forward." Stand still. Do not pray just now. March. It was the command of God that they go forward, and then by faith they went. All murmuring hushed for the moment because of what Moses had said and done. The command of God, while those in advance of the people watched and waited and wondered. After their grumbling they saw the road stretching over the sea. They were conscious of the springing up of the wind, and they watched the waters which had prevented all possibility of progress, rolling back, rolling back until they were piled in a crystal heap, and a road was left, dry—that they might pass over dry-shod. By faith they marched.

Yes, they still needed faith. I cannot help it. I am bound to let myself have my own way. I wonder if they did not wonder if the wind would turn and become west. There the waters are. They are piled up. It is a dry way, but the waters may come back. God had commanded, and, however tremblingly they marched, and the record says: "The children of Israel went into the midst of the sea upon the dry ground; and the waters were a wall unto them on their right hand, and on their left." I watch them march, march, march until they are all over; and then I listen, and they are all singing, and you know the version of their song set to a hymn, not in our hymn-book:

> "Sound the loud timbrel o'er Egypt's dark sea,
> Jehovah hath conquered, His people are free."

We still hear the song. Now watch that crowd; every move was actuated by faith, not certainty, not knowledge, not even assurance in the full sense of the word, but by faith, adventure, a venture based upon the command of God. By faith they left Egypt, crossed over the sea, and their faith was vindicated in the fact that they obeyed in spite of their own doubt. In spite of their own murmuring they marched, and they reached the other shore.

Then we have forty years to look at. Because their faith failed, they were wandering up and down in the wilderness. Have you ever tried to trace the journeyings from the Bible? You can see how they went, hither and thither through "that great and terrible wilderness"—I am quoting Moses—forty years because their faith failed; but still onward, still believing in God, under the discipline of God. Now the forty years have passed away, and again we see them. They crossed the Jordan, and the crossing of the Jordan was again a supernatural intervention as was the crossing of the Red Sea. We read of the effect upon the kings of the nations surrounding, created by the fact that this strange people had crossed the Jordan dry-shod. Joshua tells us:

"It came to pass, when all the kings of the Amorites, which were beyond Jordan westward, and all the kings of the Canaanites, which were by the sea, heard how that the Lord had dried up the waters of Jordan from before the children of Israel, until we were passed over, that their heart melted, neither was there spirit in them any more, because of the children of Israel."

Then they advanced into the land, and the story that I read is the story of how they surrounded the first city. Jericho was the first city they met, and they were there by the command of God to take possession of the land, and there were the walls of Jericho confronting them. Now what is the story? It is the story of the activity of faith, faith in obedience to a Divine order—one pauses, and has to speak carefully, and yet I speak resolutely—a Divine order which apparently had no connection whatever with the taking of a city, and the falling of its walls, and the opening of its gates. The Lord simply told them they were to take the Ark, and go round the city, the priests blowing trumpets; and they were to do it one day, and the next day, and the next, six days; and on the seventh they were to do it seven times. Do you see any—yes, I nearly said it—do you see any sense in it? Is there anything rational in that? Marching round the wall of a city, blowing horns, with a Box at the centre, which they called an Ark? I say without any hesitation, apparently there was no energy, no power, no force in what they were doing.

But they did it by faith, and by faith they were silent. If we read that sixth chapter a little earlier than at the point where I began, we shall find they were commanded to keep silence, tramping, tramping, tramping, no human voice raised; nothing but the blasting of the horns. Is anything going to happen? I cannot tell what they thought. I know what they did. They marched, they marched, they marched until at the seventh day they were told no longer to cease, or refrain from shouting, but to shout. There went up a great shout, and lo! the walls before them crumbled. I am quite careless about the modern idea that an earthquake caused the walls to fall, and that they try to prove the earthquake. Probably there was one, but *God* caused the earthquake. All I know is they marched and marched, and the walls fell. The silent people, the marching priests, the great shout, every move actuated by faith. Such are the two incidents quoted about the history of these people and their faith.

I take the whole story, indeed all the story of this eleventh chapter, if you like, specially fixing my thinking for a moment upon this, and I say that I learn as I watch and listen, and have the interpretation of this letter that faith acts when there is no explanation in sight. That is always what faith does, and often it acts when the acts have no reasonable grounds. That is true in both of these incidents. There is no reasonable explanation as to how to get away from Pi-hahiroth and Egypt. There is no reasonable explanation of the city yielding. Remember when faith acts, it is not faith does the work. It is faith makes possible the activity of God. The results are the acts of God in their advance upon the sea, dividing it. Not the tramping of feet shook the walls of Jericho down. God divided the sea. God cast down the walls of Jericho, but in order to

7

do it, these people had to obey, and it was the obedience of faith. Faith by obedience prepares the way for the activities of God. His commands are so constantly seen to be beyond the reason; but His commands are always intended to fling us back upon Himself. It was in the hour when they could do nothing either in front of the Red Sea, or in front of the walls of Jericho, but what He said, they were flung back upon God; then it was possible for Him to act. Such is the story of beginnings.

Then comes the appalling history to which I have made reference at the beginning, and thus it is a history full of solemn warnings. The people who so began, became at last a generation faithless and perverse, and so blinded by their faithlessness and perversity that they crucified the Lord of glory. Without attempting to answer it, I am tempted to use, yet in another connection, the question Paul put to the Galatians: "Ye were running well; who did hinder you?" What did hinder them? What spoiled them? What degraded their faith? And again I shall quote, and quote a word written for us as well as for those very Hebrew Christians from which the story I am touching upon is taken. Listen:

"Take heed, brethren, lest haply there shall be in any one of you an evil heart of unbelief, in falling away from the living God."

That is how they failed. That is why they failed, "in falling away from the living God." Such is the story.

Someone has said—you have all read it and know it is true— that by-products are always valuable things. For instance the by-products of coal are wonderful things. We know this, that if we really knew the value of the by-products of coal it would be a penal thing to burn coal in an open grate. All right, you are mostly warmed otherwise to-day. What are you talking about? you ask me. Well, the by-products of these stories are very wonderful, and as I ponder over these stories my reluctance to look at them is overcome, and my prayer was and is that there may be something in them for me, and for those to whom I speak. Every action which is not of faith, but which is a venture, may lead to uttermost disaster. We may take an action, which appears to be exactly what the people of faith are doing, but if not an action of faith, it may lead to disaster; "Which the Egyptians assaying to do were swallowed up." They were trying to do exactly what these people had done, not in faith, but taking a risk. Surely the water will remain long enough for us to get over. There is nothing sure about it if you shut God out. Actions which appear to be actions of faith, but which are not based on faith, may lead to uttermost and terrific disaster, "Which the Egyptians assaying to do were drowned."

Then I come to this other story, and I do not forget that things follow the story which have their bearings upon it; and the second of the things that I am venturing to call the by-products of these stories is this, that faith must have its actions completed in obedience, or disaster will follow. Where do we get that? Well read on. There was one man, a member of the nation, who broke the law of God when in Jericho. He saw a Babylonish garment and a wedge of gold, and he coveted them; and they were strictly charged there was to be no looting, and he has it in his tent, and the whole march was defeated at Ai until the thing was discovered and put right, and the sin was cleansed away. It is not enough for the first vision that must come, but it must be obedient, and it must conform to all the commandments of God. By faith they—poor, stupid people, nevertheless for the moment acting by faith—left Egypt, crossed the sea, took the city of Jericho, and began the conquest of the land.

XV

The Faith of Rahab

SCRIPTURE LESSON - - Joshua ii. 1-21; vi. 22-25

"By faith Rahab the harlot perished not with them that were
disobedient"   Hebrews xi. 31

As we study this wonderful record of the triumphs of faith
in the letter to the Hebrews, it is inevitable that we find ourselves
sharply pulled up by this text. Looking at faith, we have seen it
illustrated in a remarkable and wonderful way in great personalities—
Abel, Enoch, Noah, Abraham, Isaac, Jacob, Joseph, Moses, the
nation leaving Egypt, the nation entering Canaan. Now suddenly,
quite definitely, with almost startling brutality, "Rahab, the harlot."

Such an amazing statement demands consideration. In passing
I may say it is rather interesting to those who are given to the
study of the Word of God, in order to its interpretation, and are
always interested and mostly helped by the opinions of other
writers (I said mostly), to see how very busy some expositors have
appeared to be in their anxiety to get rid of this verse. They have
tried to explain it away somehow. It is not long since I was reading
an article by a very brilliant writer, a preacher, who came to this
story, and by the time I had finished reading his article I was quite
sure the thing had never happened! Of course I went back to my
Bible as the ultimate court of appeal in all these matters. Let us
remember first of all that the reference of the writer of the letter
to the Hebrews is to a definite historic event; and in the second
place that what he says is an inspired interpretation of that event.
This is an event in history. The story is from the book of Joshua,
and in this letter of the Hebrews, the writer thinking of faith,
writing of faith, illustrating faith, having moved through this
wonderful list of outstanding personalities, writes down, without
any apology, "Rahab the harlot perished not with them that were
disobedient." If this statement is startling, marking her for all
time, it therefore demands consideration, and to that I propose we
give ourselves. First let us look at this woman; then consider her
faith; and finally consider the issues of that faith.

First the woman herself, and I am principally concerned with

100

14-938

this whole story, as it constitutes a revelation of God. Of course
the woman is here. We are told what she did, and we are going
to look at what she did, and of course it had its issues. But the
great revelation is one of God, and it is the more remarkable that
it blazes out in that Old Testament history, when comparatively
even those who believed in the One God, were living in the twilight,
when they lacked the clear shining of the light given to us in which
to live. Now the New Testament writer, when the twilight has
given place to the dawning and rising of the sun, quotes from that
Old Testament record, and I hope we shall see what an unveiling
of God is here, even in that dim distance of the past.

Who was this woman? First remember that she was a pagan.
Having said that, perhaps I need not say any more, but I am going
to say more. We are terribly prone to put the measurement of
the light in which we live on past events, and to judge people
in the light in which it is our privilege to walk. It is not fair,
right, or reasonable. Before we come to any hasty conclusion,
remember that she was a pagan. She belonged to those people
who dwelt in Canaan. We find her described in the Old Testament
in Joshua, and in the New, in my text, and in James by this ex-
tremely ugly word "harlot." It is true that the Hebrew word
so rendered may simply mean an inn-keeper, and several Jewish
expositors so explain her, and almost invariably describe her as
an inn-keeper. But it is interesting that the translators in the
Greek, the Septuagint, employ a word that does not bear that
interpretation, a word that we associate with our word harlot;
and it is equally significant that when the writer of the letter to
the Hebrews, and James in his letter made reference to her, they
employ the word, the Greek word that the Septuagint translators
had used. I think there is no doubt that the word is justified, and
we have the story, "Rahab, the harlot."

But we need to remember some other things. Even if we
understand the word as we use it to-day, the dire and sorrowful
and terrible word it connotes, we must not measure that woman
by our standards. First of all she lived in a land where the worship was inevitably pagan. There were various gods and god-
desses; and in all the worship of that country there was the
deification of natural forces, especially the sexual. Nearly all their
worship circled around that terrific mystery, and religion consisted
in giving license to appetite. Here this woman was born, and
here she had lived. If her manner of life was indeed, as we believe
it was, described by the terrible word used, then in that country

and city and time, among those people it was tolerated. Nay, toleration is too weak a word. It was encouraged, she was looked upon not as irreligious, but rather as a priestess. I am trying to visualize the picture, and that means this, to summarize. This woman had no consciousness of sin, and no consciousness of holiness, as these two great facts were given to those people of Israel to know and to understand.

She had no consciousness of sin. Oh, I think very likely, as in the case of all men everywhere shrouded in darkness, there was a consciousness of the difference between right and wrong; but certainly that consciousness would not enter into the living of the life this woman was living. Sin? No one would have called her a sinner among the people of which she was a member. Holiness? They did not understand the term. It was a term not known among these pagan peoples. These two opposites were not seen as they were seen by the Jewish people. That came through the law of Moses. So we have this woman living in a pagan atmosphere, brought up in the worship—if there was worship at all—of the deification of natural forces, and especially in the sexual forces; a woman ministering to her age.

It is very difficult to see this and to understand it. Here we are as to date, in 1943, which has to do with the coming of Jesus, and the revolution in human thinking that has been wrought by Him; and the interpretation by Him of the meaning of sin and holiness. That is where we are living, and if the word harlot is whispered, almost inevitably there is created in our mind a sense of horror. We have all sorts of names, and I hardly like to defile my lips, but there they are—prostitute. I do not know why you reserve that word for the woman and not for the man! Fallen woman we say. I am not quarrelling with it, but I am saying those attitudes are the result of the light in which we are living. This woman had none of them: a pagan, a woman outside the covenant, without the law, with no consciousness of sin or of holiness, or of the difference between them.

There was something fine about her. We cannot read this story quite simply and naturally, without bias and prejudice, without seeing that she had got a heart, and in view of the perils that were threatening her people she thought of father and mother and brothers and sisters. Do not pass that over lightly. There is always something fine to be discovered in the most depraved people. I may get all the theologians down on me now! You may say, Don't you believe in total depravity? I do not. Don't you believe in original sin? I do, because I have found so much in myself, and in so many of you! Listen to one word of Jesus that lights up the whole thought. He was talking to blasphemers, to His enemies, to those all round about Him opposed to Him and His words, and He said: "If ye then, being evil, know how to give good gifts unto your children." That is all I want. Do you see the recognition. You are evil, but there is something good in you. You know how to give good gifts to your children. That is a truth never to be forgotten, that however depraved a man or woman may be, they are good to their children. Here it is seen away back in the Old Testament. Think of my father, think of my mother, think of my brothers and sisters. Her's was not a selfish nature altogether. At any rate there was something in it that is fine. There is the woman. Did I hear a whisper that I am white-washing her? I am not. I am taking off the black smudge men have placed upon her, and asking you to see her in the light of her age, with no consciousness of sin and of holiness, brought up in the midst of religious rites and ceremonies that all seemed to warrant her in the very life she was leading. That is the woman, Rahab the harlot.

Then we have the story of her faith, and how it acted. First of all her faith was founded upon a conviction that had come to her concerning the people that were approaching, and the secrets of the approach of these people. Notice what she told those spies, that they were familiar with the advance of this people of Israel as they crossed the Red Sea. That is a very significant thing. The crossing of the Red Sea had been forty years before, and it is quite possible that this woman was not living then. But mark the effect it had on all these peoples of Canaan. She heard about it, heard the old men talking of that march of the host dry shod through the parted waters of the Red Sea, into the wilderness. It had produced a fear and terror in the minds of the people.

Moreover she referred to the fact of the victories won over Sihon and Og. Go back to Numbers to get all the particulars. Here is the conviction that possessed her own soul. I give it in her own words: "The Lord your God, He is God in heaven above, and on earth beneath." It was a wonderful declaration. Born and bred in that pagan atmosphere, and trained in that way, acting in accordance with those earlier religious blasphemies—she would not have called them that—but she had come to see behind this strange people who crossed the sea on dry land, and overcame two mighty enemies who opposed their progress, she had come to see God, had come to the conviction that behind the people was One other, and that One other was God.

Now on the basis of that conviction her faith took action. What was it? First of all an appeal, then a venture, and then obedience. I am not going to discuss this old story as to what she said. We may say she did not tell the truth. I do not think we must talk about that in this country when we think of war time, and of propaganda. We need to be careful. Remember the day again. I have heard clever interpretations of this, that when she said the spies had gone out, they had gone out—on to the roof! I am not prepared to take that line of interpretation. Undoubtedly she acted untruthfully, or she said things that were not exactly so. But I am not concerned with that. Her heart was filled with fear at the approach of these people, and with greater fear because she had become convinced that Someone was behind them, and the Someone was the God of heaven and the God of earth; and she made an appeal to His representatives for pity.

The Revised Version reads: "Rahab the harlot perished not with them that were disobedient." I am not quarrelling with the Old Version that says "them that believed not," because not to believe is to be disobedient. They also had heard of the crossing of the Red Sea. They also had known of the victories over Sihon and Og. They also had had the fact of the mysterious God forced upon them, but they had not obeyed it. They were disobedient, and they persisted in their own courses. Here is this woman venturing, venturing, venturing, and she was obedient. That is faith. "By faith Rahab the harlot perished not." Here I cannot refrain from pointing out that it is an arresting word that the writer of the letter to the Hebrews uses, this letter which is pre-eminently one of faith; and the letter of James which is said to be the letter of works. Both writers quote this woman. One says, "By faith Rahab," and the other says, "Rahab . . . justified by works." They are both true. We see her faith operating in obedience.

What is the essence of all that? A soul in pagan darkness coming upon the fact of God, yielding to the fact, and acting on behalf of the purposes of God. She had come into contact with that God as she hid the spies, and as she appealed for mercy. That was the act of faith, and it was a great act. I do not want to be putting these things into comparison. It is very absurd to try and do it. We look back over the chapter, Abel, Enoch, Noah, Abraham, Isaac, Jacob, Joseph and Moses. Not one of them was more remarkable in faith than was this pagan woman who, coming upon the fact of God, went out, yielding an obedience to the thing of which she was convinced, and flung herself upon Him through His representatives, seeking for deliverance.

Then finally, in a word, what were the issues? We all know. She and all her family were preserved. Did you notice that remarkable little phrase in the sixth chapter of Joshua? "She dwelt in the midst of Israel, unto this day." Of course that is the day in which the story was written. We see what happened. She was delivered, and was put outside the camp for a while, and then was admitted into the national life of this people, and she dwelt from that day forward in Israel. In other words, she became a daughter of Israel. She cast in her lot with them in worship and life. One could let one's imagination run riot. I can imagine how at first she had to be instructed, had to be told the meaning of sin, and light flung upon her past life. She had to know the meaning of holiness, but she dwelt in Israel unto this day, and cast in her lot with the people of God in worship and in life. That is all we know about her in the Old Testament.

When we get into the New Testament we have another startling revelation, for not only the writer of the letter to the Hebrews, and James mention her. Matthew names her. He puts her name in a list, in the first chapter, in that great genealogical table of Jesus which was the legal genealogy, not the actual, although the lines converge at a certain point. Joseph adopted Jesus, "being as was supposed the son of Joseph." That is a poor translation. It is, "being by legal adoption the son of Joseph." It was necessary the name of Jesus should be entered in the archives. Luke gives us the actual genealogy through Mary. Matthew's is the legal, and if we look down it we find this amazing thing. It is a Jewish genealogy, and yet in it we find five women. Luke's is also a Jewish genealogy, but he names no women. Listen to the women Matthew names: Tamar, Rahab, Ruth, Bathsheba, Mary. Tamar, the story of her sin is terrific. Rahab, the harlot. Ruth shines with brightness and beauty. Bathsheba, we know her story. Rahab is named, and finds her place. Mark where she comes. She is the wife of Salmon, and Salmon begat Boaz, and Boaz begat Obed, and Obed begat Jesse, and Jesse begat David. Go on and on, and you will come to Jesus. Through Rahab, indirectly, came the Messiah. Oh, I know people have difficulties about Salmon as to who he was. There was a quaint Scotch expositor who thought he was one of the spies, and that Rahab married him. At any rate there is the issue, a pagan woman making a venture under conviction, delivered as the result of her venture, dwelling in Israel, becoming a daughter of these very people, coming to look on life as they did, marrying into the nation, presently dying, and we know nothing more. The ages sweep on and on, until at last Jesus. "By faith Rahab the harlot."

Fifteen hundred years after this historic incident Peter was one day speaking, and telling of a new view that had come to him of life and humanity. What did he say?

"Of a truth I perceive that God is no Respecter of persons, but in every nation he that feareth Him, and worketh righteousness, is acceptable to Him."

It took fifteen hundred years, and then almost reluctantly, and with difficulty an apostle of Jesus Christ came to see that. Well, here it is away back, fifteen hundred years before, God no Respecter of persons, of countenances. Joshua and his massed hosts made no appeal to Him because of their countenances, because that is the word Peter used. There is a woman who was convinced and wrought righteousness by faith, she was acceptable to Him. God is revealed to us here, one of the gleams full of glory, shining in the Old Testament.

When we are tempted to look with contempt upon any human being for any reason whatsoever, let us remember Rahab, and let us form our estimates of human beings not on the basis of a past, which may have been one of definite iniquity and sin, and more often is one due to ignorance and wrong up-bringing; but let us base our conception upon that present attitude; and if they too, out of the midst of all these things, with only a glimmering of light as yet, not understanding all the mighty things of our faith and holiness, have nevertheless made contact with Him and submit to Him by faith, like Rahab they are delivered, and perish not.

XVI

The Faith of Others

THESE words are selected from the penultimate paragraph of this chapter or section concerning faith. The story does not end with this chapter, but runs over into the twelfth. The whole section began in chapter ten with the declaration of the great principle: "My righteous one shall live by faith," or as the old rendering had it: "The just shall live by faith." The writer later defined faith as conviction of things hoped for, and consciousness of unseen things. It has proceeded after that enunciation of a principle, and that definition of faith to illustrate the triumphs of faith, first of all in racial history: Abel, Enoch, Noah; and then in Hebrew history: Abraham, Isaac, Jacob, Joseph, Moses, the whole nation, and Rahab.

The section now draws to a conclusion in a passage which is an impetuous summary of persons and deeds. This summary is vibrant with power, poignant in its account of sufferings, and challenging in its revelation of triumph. These three little sentences are indices, enabling us to focus the suggestiveness of the entire paragraph, and we take them as constituting our divisions. First, "Time will fail me." Secondly, "Of whom the world was not worthy." Thirdly, "These all . . . received not the promise."

"The time will fail me." There is a temptation to take the names and deal with them one by one. After all, we have no more time than the writer had, and therefore I cannot better his method. There is something very suggestive in the fact that at the close he grouped names, and then deeds. He says: "The time will fail me" to deal with them, and he gives a list of names. "The time will fail me." What does he mean?

It means first of all that the list he has given is not exhaustive. He has not named all the names. He has illustrated faith. By no means has he exhausted the theme. The principle has operated through a succession of persons and deeds through all the running centuries at which this writer was casting a backward look, as he was writing to those Christians who were in danger of being weakened, as they felt they had lost so much, as they had to turn their back on the splendours of the Hebrew ritual, and to be content with the simplicities in Christ. To that end he is showing them the power of faith, the great thing in the history of men, not the ritual and the ceremony, but the principle of faith. This little phrase, which can be dealt with and dismissed, says: This is not an exhaustive list. There have been persons all through human history, persons who lived and wrought by faith, deeds which had been the actual outcome of this principle of faith. The principle has operated through a succession of persons and deeds; and now the writer says: I could go on, but time fails me.

Let us pause a moment with the list, the illustration first of persons, and then of experiences, the persons actuated by faith. Look over the list again, and see the selections are reminiscent. They are not chronological. He has not come down the ages, naming the persons chronologically. He seems to have a mind filled with the past, and he names them without reference to chronology. Yet there is a system. He names five judges—Gideon, Barak, Samson, Jephthah, Samuel. He names one king, and only one—David. Then he groups in one phrase, that brilliant succession—"the prophets." Evidently in the back of the writer's mind was this process of history, a continuous stream in history.

It is interesting to look over the list and think it out in many ways. First of all, notice that faith seems to have been pre-eminently manifested in the time of the Judges. Some names are there over which one ponders and wonders when we read them. We know the stories behind them, Gideon; oh, yes. Barak, of course, the statesman who stood by Deborah. Samson, yes, he is named, and we shall have to leave him in the list. Jephthah, oh yes, a man who suffered iniquitous disability because born out of wedlock, and the iron had entered his soul, but he was a great man. Samuel, well, of course. Thus in the period of the Judges this writer groups five names. We know what followed them. Saul, David, Solomon, and then an appalling succession; the kingdom rent in twain, Israel and Judah, king succeeded king. Of these he only names one. That is not to say there were no others that acted on the principle of faith. I would include Hezekiah. But looking over the period of the history, he sees faith operating more strikingly in the period of the Judges than in that of the Kings. Then beyond the kings, during their kingship, the period when God ceased to speak to the kings, and spake through prophets only, and to the kings through the prophets, he groups all the prophets in one. Faith is seen to be a continuous principle. Illustrations abound. He has given a wonderful selection, but the list is not exhaustive. Faith has been there, operating in individuals, and he gives illustrations, some astonishing us, but they are there, "through faith."

Then he passes to that passage which I often wish I knew how to read. I love reading the Bible, and reading the Bible in public. I never read it here until I have read it again and again at home in preparation. I have been going over this passage again, and am impressed by the marvel of it, the pathway of suffering endurance, the pathway of constant triumph. Through faith, kingdoms subdued, righteousness wrought, promises obtained, the mouth of lions stopped, the power of fire quenched, the edge of the sword escaped, strength proceeding out of weakness. In war, mighty, turning to flight armies of aliens. Then that tender poignant word, occurring in the midst, "Women received their dead by a resurrection." But he has by no means done.

"Others were tortured, not accepting their deliverance; that they might obtain a better resurrection; and others had trial of mockings and scourgings"; and as I read I am inclined to think the mockings are harder to bear than the scourgings. I do not know.

"Yea, moreover of bonds and imprisonment; they were stoned, they were sawn asunder, they were tempted, they were slain with the sword; they went about in sheepskins, in goatskins; being destitute, afflicted, evil entreated (of whom the world was not worthy)." What a story. What a survey of history, and of things that happened in history. Yes, Russell Lowell was right:

"Truth for ever on the scaffold, Wrong for ever on the throne,
   Yet that scaffold sways the future, and, behind the dim unknown
   Standeth God within the shadow, keeping watch above His own."

The deeds of faith, the sufferings of faith, the enduring of faith. So he summarizes; and time will fail to tell, every phrase a story, every sentence having behind it something of history, but showing what faith has made men able to endure; faith triumphant through agony down the running ages. Such is the summary.

Then we come to the second little phrase. How very suggestive it is in parenthesis. Now he has gone beyond the people to the deeds which I have read again, and he is looking at the people who endured; and in a pregnant phrase he says: "Of whom the world was not worthy." The world. That of course is the world order, the order of life in which these people endured, the order of life which created the opposition to these people, and created their own suffering, so that they endured, and bore, and patiently went on. The world!

What were the characteristics of the world? First of all, no consciousness of things not seen. To put that more briefly, in a word, godless. Secondly, no conviction of things hoped for, the hopeless world. But that in a phrase, without God, and therefore without hope. The world. Oh yes, this is all past history. The writer has been quoting from past history, but the description abides. That is the world, that has no consciousness of things not seen, the world that smiles with a sort of superior air of pity upon any man who prays; the world that if you tell them you are going to a prayer meeting, of course looks at you quite pleasantly, and yet thinks what a fool you are. The world has no consciousness of things unseen, no traffic with the eternal, no dealing with the undying ages, no sense of God—the world!

If it be true that such is the condition of the world, it is equally true that they have no conviction of things hoped for. Things are hoped for, but they have no certainty. They are hoping for many things. They are hoping for peace, but they are not sure that there will be peace. They are hoping for the things of the dust, things of the earth, but they have no guarantee; and the pessimism of our common literature to-day is evidence of the hopelessness of godlessness. The writer here says all these people lived in the midst of these things, and they triumphed. Therefore these people constituted the world's true wealth. The world was not worthy of them. The world from the standpoint of value was not comparable to these people; the world that hated, and opposed, and caused suffering. But the people who were opposed, who endured the suffering, constituted the world's true wealth.

It has always been so. We may pass back over this whole chapter again, and think of what the world owes to these men. Go back to Abel. We do not know very much of what the world owes to him. Enoch? Let that pass. Noah? What about Abraham? What does the world owe to him? What does the world owe to Moses? I grant you I am taking out the peaks of personality, but it is not only true of them. It is true of all these others and of those whose names are not written, but of whom deeds are recounted; those who suffered, those who in the power of faith stood true and loyal to their convictions, those who were convinced of things unseen, as constituting the supreme reality in life, those who were certain of things they hoped for, that one day, as Browning has it, "though a wide compass round be fetched," the victory will come; those are the men and women who are contributing to anything worth while in human history. "Of whom the world was not worthy."

That brings us to the last of these sentences. The writer says at the close, "These all"—Abel, Enoch, Noah, Abraham, all of them; time will fail me to tell of a group which he named—these all, whose names are not written, but whose deeds are recounted, well, what of them? "These all . . . received not the promise." Now I submit to you that is a most startling and challenging statement, and I am inclined to ask at first, what does this mean? Has faith failed? Is the story of faith the story of failure from beginning to end? They endured, they suffered, they bore their testimony, they lived by faith, they built upon faith, they died; but not one of them had received the promise. I repeat, that is a challenging statement.

We are at once driven to ask this. What does the writer mean by "the promise"? "They . . . received not the promise." Think of all these men of faith, beginning, let us say, with Abraham, or even going back to the man Abel, who by faith sang the first solo of redemption in the glory. Go through them all, they received not the promise. What does it mean? Was it all wrong? Did they die and miss the way? Certainly not. What then is meant by "the promise"? Here I make a statement which you can verify for yourselves at your leisure. The idea of the promise runs all through this great epistle, occurring no less than eighteen times. What does the word mean? The word "promise" means an announcement which is a pledge. They all died, not having received the fulfilment of the pledge which had been announced to them, the very pledge that constituted the basis of their faith. They died, they had not received the promise.

Let us press that a little further. The promise was the word of God, and the pledge of God, upon which faith builds. What was it, what was the promise that supported Abraham? Go through the chapter, and certain references make it perfectly clear what the promise was. Abraham "looked for the city which hath the foundations, whose Builder and Maker is God." How do we understand that? Go a little further down the chapter: "They are seeking after a country of their own . . . they desire a better country, that is a heavenly." Does that mean heaven? That certainly does not mean heaven. They were seeking a city. They died not having reached the city. They were seeking a country, a country of their own, a country where they could breathe the air, a country where they could realize all the beauties of life; but they never reached it. They were seeking a better country, a heavenly, that is a country on earth, according to the heavenly order.

Take these three sentences in their setting and reference, and what were these people seeking? They were not seeking to get to heaven. Abraham did not leave Ur of Chaldea in the hope that one day he would arrive in heaven. These people who endured and suffered and witnessed through the running ages, were not seeking to gain heaven. What were they seeking? Not that they should gain heaven, but that God should gain earth. To run over to Revelation: go home and read the twenty-first chapter again, and read of that city. We take that wonderful chapter, and make beautiful hymns about it, "Jerusalem the Golden," and all the time we are looking up and thinking about heaven. It is not heaven at all. It is the establishment in the world of the Divine order. What did Jesus tell His disciples to pray, and what do we pray for in obedience to the command? "Our Father, Who art in the heavens." I pause to say that is a plural word, "heavens," which it ought to be. A doctrine of the omnipresence of God is there. He is in all the heavens. "Our Father, Who art in the heavens, Thy name be hallowed, Thy Kingdom come, Thy will be done on earth, as it is in heaven." That is the true passion of the man of faith. See how that ending to this wonderful chapter lifts faith into the highest and truest realm.

What is your faith? Is it purely individual? Is it entirely personal? Is it an activity that is bringing blessing to your own soul? Then it is a poor thing. Faith only becomes majestic and supreme when it realises the ultimate purpose of God for this earth and for humanity; and the promise that they did not receive was that God had reserved "some better thing" for us, that they without us "should not be made perfect."

Therefore, "seeing we are compassed about with so great a cloud of witnesses"—that does not mean the people who are watching us, but that they are talking to us, bearing witness to the power of faith—"seeing we are compassed about with so great a cloud of witnesses, let us lay aside every weight, and the sin which doth so easily beset us." I do not like that translation, "the sin which doth so easily beset." It is one Greek one, *euperistaton*, which means the sin that is in good standing around. Is there such a

thing as a sin in good standing around? What is it? Unbelief.
Did you ever know a Society formed asking men to sign a pledge,
or promise that they will not believe. Some people seem to think
that intellectually they are not up to date if they are not shot through
with unbelief of some sort. We are to lay aside that which con-
tradicts faith. Let us lay aside every weight. What are the weights?
The things that hinder us running. Will I name some? No, I
will not. Why not? I should name something that is a weight to
me, that would not be to you. Perhaps I will name one. What is
it? Trying to find out what the other man's weights are! Lay
aside the weights, the things that hinder in the race that is being run,
through peril, toil, and pain oftentimes in the history of humanity.
Laying them aside let us run with patience the race set before us.

He did not finish there. What follows is the final interpretation.
"Looking unto Jesus, the Author and Perfecter of faith." I want
to emphasise that closing statement, that seems to suggest failure
of faith, but does nothing of the kind. Faith is co-operation with
God in the interest of the consummation upon which the heart of
God is set. "They had witness borne to them through their faith,"
and they marched toward the goal which has not yet been reached.
We are still marching toward it. The circumstances have varied,
but the march is the same and the principle is the same.

Remember that all the illustrations that we have in this chapter,
up to this closing part, are prior to Christ. All these people lived
by faith without the knowledge of Christ. With Him a new period
and a new era began, but the principle still persists, and the way of
faith is still oftentimes the way of suffering. But it is the way of
power, and it is the way of progress. Time will fail us; we can make
no complete list; it is too great. And of these, such people who do
such deeds and endure such suffering, the world is not worthy.
They still march on and on, but not yet have they received the
fulfilment of the promise. But the promise stands, the pledge is
made; and at last:

> "Though the wide compass round be fetched,
>   What began best, can't end worst";

the Kingdom of our God shall come and be established, and toward
that our faces are set, and towards that we are marching.

XVII

The Faith of the Supreme Witness

SCRIPTURE LESSON   -   -   -   Hebrews ii. 5-13; xi. 39-xii. 3
"Looking unto Jesus, the Author and Perfecter of faith."
—Hebrews xii. 2

HAVING illustrated the power of faith from the past Patriarchal and Hebrew economies, the writer of this letter did not urge these Hebrew Christians to take any of those he had mentioned as an example. Their witness is to serve as inspiration, but not as perfect pattern. Seeing the cloud of witnesses the race is to be run; and he wrote to Hebrew Christians, and indeed to all Christians, urging them to run in this self-same race. How is it to be run? "Looking unto Jesus, the Author and Finisher of faith." The reason is that only in Him has faith had its full and final interpretation in human history. I am speaking from the standpoint of His human life for the moment.

Our versions say, "Looking unto Jesus, the Author and Finisher or Perfecter of our faith." I did not read it like that. I missed out one word when I read the lesson and the text. The word *our* is not in the Greek, and the writer did not say He is the Author and Finisher or Perfecter of our faith. I am quite willing to admit that it is wonderfully true that He is the Author of my faith, and I believe by grace He will be the Perfecter of my faith, but that is not what the writer says here. He says He is the Author and Perfecter of faith. He is talking of the principle of faith, and declaring that is seen in Jesus. I resolutely use the name that the writer of the letter uses, in spite of the view held by some that we ought never to use the name in that way. That is a view with which I have no sympathy at all. This writer does not say the Lord Jesus Christ. All that is true, and true of Him. It has recently been said when we think of Him we should think with all reverence, and we cannot do so if we say Jesus. I do not understand that conception. I am speaking of Him as this writer does so constantly, Jesus; and in my thinking of Him is everything of awe and reverence.

The writer of the letter says, "Looking unto Jesus," and the human name is very significant in its interpretation in this writing, and specially in this phrase. "Looking unto Jesus, the Author." What is the meaning of "Author"? What is the real meaning of the word that the writer used here? It does not mean originator. I will give his word in a literal English translation. It may seem to lose something for the moment. "Looking unto Jesus the File-Leader," that is to say, the One Who takes precedence, the One Who is Head of the great procession, leading it in revelation. As we have tried to follow through this wonderful section, beginning in the tenth chapter, running through the eleventh, and culminating in the twelfth, we have seen marvellous illustrations of faith. Yes, says the writer, it is a wonderful procession that spans the ages from Abel down, coming to Jesus; but look, and you will see one Personality Who moves past the whole of them and stands at the head. He is the File-Leader, He is the Author in that sense. He is the File-Leader, the One Who has pre-eminence. And Vindicator, Perfecter; yes, but the word means the One Who vindicates the principle, the One Who supremely reveals it in its working. He is the File-Leader and the One Whose revelation of it in its working is the final vindication of the principle in all human life. These are the technicalities to which I referred.

But now glance back with me for a moment. In every illustration fear results in failure at certain times and in certain places. There is not one of all those named—and I was careful to show he did not name all—he said, "time would fail me"—and almost haphazard, he gives us a group of names. Take them and go through those he deals with more particularly, there is no single illustration that is perfect. In Abel there is no story of sin or failure, but his blood sacrifice suggests his consciousness of failure and imperfection, while at the same time it cancelled it. Enoch walked with God, but he did not live the perfect life of faith, for the first sixty years he lived on the ordinary and mediocre level of his times. Noah fell into actual sin. Abraham more than once turned aside from the simple pathway of faith. Isaac became degenerate and fleshly. Jacob had to be crippled in order to be finally victorious. Joseph was unable to accomplish the deliverance he foresaw, and was buried in a coffin in Egypt. Moses was excluded from the land of promise because he spake unadvisedly with his lips. The nation utterly broke down in its testimony to God. Rahab had a past of paganism, so that her life was not wholly complete. Each of the judges named, and all judges, were guilty of faltering, to say the least, at certain points. David committed sin of the deepest dye. The prophets, those wonderful men, faltered often for lack of perfect sympathy with God and man; and for the rest, no absolute victory was ever won in individual life, and through all suffering the deepest depth was never reached.

Therefore, because there has been no perfect illustration of the principle, the writer draws attention to One which is perfect and complete and final. "Looking unto Jesus." Notice this picture of our Lord occurs in the midst of an injunction.

"Therefore, let us also, seeing we are compassed about with so great a cloud of witnesses."

That does not mean people who are watching us, in spite of popular and long continued exposition. When a boy I well remember hearing sermons on that text, and wonderful sermons they would have been if they had been true that it meant this, that we are running a race, and if it does not vulgarise the story, they are stretching over the battlements of heaven, and are watching to see how we do. But they are not watching us. They are witnessing to us, talking to us. The examples of the past are eloquent with force and the fertility of faith.

"Therefore, . . . seeing we are compassed about with so great a cloud of witnesses, let us lay aside every weight, and the sin that is in good standing around, and let us run with patience the race that is set before us."

We are not to do so, keeping our eye upon Abel and Enoch and Noah and Abraham! What then are we to do? "Looking unto Jesus." We are to see the witnesses, we are to listen to them. We are to listen to the testimony of their lives which gives force and fertility to faith, but we are to look to Him.

"Looking," to stay again with a technicality. The Greek word is very remarkable. It occurs nowhere else in the New Testament. There are so many words that speak of vision, but this word is peculiar. It has a quantity in it that is in no other word. It has an adverbial prefix. I am not familiar with every translation, and only know one—there may be others—that really gives the effect of the Greek word. It is not the Authorised or Revised, nor the American Revision. It is not Moffatt, but it is Weymouth's, which, from the standpoint of personal and individual translation, I hold to be the greatest ever done by an individual of the New Testament. How does Weymouth translate? "Looking off unto Jesus." It is a curious thing that little word "off," which is the translation of the prefix. "Looking off," what does it mean? The root idea of the word is one that expresses the fact that there is a vision which will surprise, a vision which will capture, a vision that will master; and it emphasizes what I am trying to say here. We are not to fix our eyes upon the saints of the past either in the old economy or the new. We are to look off from them, "looking off unto Jesus."

That word is enough to hold us for a long time. I am not going to stay, but there have been times when I have wished that the lives of the saints had never been written. They are often very discouraging. They are not helpful always. They have their values. I have read with great delight the story of Madame Guyon and others of the mystic saints; but they are very disappoint- and discouraging. Look off, quit looking at these saints of the past. Quit looking at the saints of the Christian era. Quit looking at the saints that you know. Look off; there is one point where the vision may be perfectly satisfied, "Looking off unto Jesus."

Now, I am not concerned with the whole of the context. The picture occurs in the midst of a great injunction. We have only to do with the picture itself. "Looking off unto Jesus." He is presented definitely, but He is qualified. Our vision has to be limited. We are to look at Him in a certain way. How? We are to see Him as the File-Leader of faith; and we are to see Him as the Vindicator of faith. Already I feel that this marvellous page, with Abel and Enoch and Noah and Abraham and David, and all of them, fades into insignificance. Let us try and do three things quite briefly; first of all ponder this description of Jesus, then consider in the context the consciousness of Jesus which produces the picture; and finally note—not staying with it—the victory of Jesus resulting from the facts revealed in the picture and the consciousness.

Of faith He is the File-Leader. I need hardly stay longer with that, but it is the arresting fact. If we glance back again at the others, we see Abel worshipping, and Enoch walking, and Noah working by faith in God. Now look at Jesus as Worshipper, as the One Who walked with God, as One Who worked with God; and we see at once how He moves to the head of the procession. He is the File-Leader.

We looked at Abraham, that great figure, and we noticed as we did his obedience, his obtaining, and his offering; and then we turn our eyes off, and look at Jesus, marking His obedience, His obtaining, and His offering. We looked at Isaac, and at the highest moments his faith was passive. The faith of Jesus was peaceful but never passive, but active. We looked at Jacob. He was restless, and he had to be pulled up again and again. Never so with

Jesus. He was always active, but never restless. Joseph at last is embalmed and put in a coffin. So is Jesus buried, but the grave could not hold Him because of what He had been in life, and what He had wrought in life, by faith. Moses was exiled from the land. Jesus entered into full possession, and even brought Moses to

> "Stand with glory wrapt around
>   On the hills he never trod,
>   And speak of the strife that won our life
>   With the Incarnate Son of God."

The judges were dictators, but how incompetent they were. The king, the one named, stands out great in many ways in leadership and as a shepherd: but when we begin to compare him with "great David's greater Son!" The prophets were forthtellers, but not one of them, or the whole of them could speak the whole truth of God. Jesus did, He was the File-Leader of faith.

But take the other statement, not only the File-Leader, but the Perfecter, which I prefer to render Vindicator. By all that has been seen in the contrast between Him and those named; by all that has been seen He is pre-eminent in His vindication of faith as a principle. There we might stay for a long time. Faith in Jesus moved from a centre out into the circumference as it always must, and as it always does in measure. But let us confine ourselves to this thought first of all, faith in God. I am not going to argue that. Read the whole story of Jesus, and we find His faith never wavered, and was characterized by true dependence upon God. What My Father gives Me that I do. His faith in God never wavered for a moment.

And that meant faith in man. Faith in man? I do not know what your opinion of man is. I do not ask for your opinion of yourself, or even of your friends, but your general conception of man. What do you think of man? I will not ask you to tell me. I will ask you to ask yourself, and answer it. Whatever you think of man, Jesus thought he was worth dying for. The Cross for evermore is the interpretation of Jesus of the value of man. What does God see in me? What does Christ see in me? The hallmark of the Divine, the possibility of human nature. He saw it beneath all the ruin and sin and shame and pollution. He believed in man. Believing in God, He believed in man.

And His faith finally was not only in God and man, it was faith in the future. You cannot find me anything, not a single note in all the sayings of Jesus, or in His outlook, which reveals pessimism.

He believed in the future. With august dignity in His final discourses, His prophetic discourses, He looked forward to that day when He would be the Judge, and the nations should be gathered before Him. He was not going to the Cross to fail but to win. "I, if I be lifted up from the earth, will draw all men unto Myself."

Faith in the future, the Vindicator of faith. How did we start our studies? With the confident declaration of the principle of life in the words, "My righteous one shall live by faith." He vindicated that principle, vindicated it in every way.

Let us press this a little, and ask how do we account for such a victory of faith? That is why I said before we need a little of the context.

"Looking unto Jesus, the Author and Perfecter of faith, Who" —now he is going to tell us the secret of His victory—"Who for the joy that was set before Him." That is the first thing. What is the next?

"Endured the Cross, despising shame." What is the last thing? "And hath sat down at the right hand of the throne of God." What an unveiling of the inner consciousness of Jesus, and what faith meant to Him.

First of all, "For the joy that was set before Him." Faith, as we saw at the very beginning, is confidence in things hoped for. Jesus had the clear vision of things hoped for; and the joy that was set before Him, what was it? The joy that filled the heart of Abraham when he left Ur of Chaldea, and went to seek a city, a country, the establishment of the city of God. Jesus went to win back the earth in its sin and wandering, and the joy set before Him was not His return to Heaven, but the fact that His return would be one of triumph, having accomplished the Divine purpose. "The joy set before Him."

Yes, but there is the shining of the ultimate glory, and the deep and profound assurance filling His heart of the final victory, there is a pathway to be trodden. "I have a baptism to be baptized with," He said, "and how am I straitened till it be accomplished." He endured the Cross, and perhaps the more reverently we leave that and say little about it the better. He endured the Cross. The Cross was a dreadful thing, a shameful thing. It was the death of a felon. It was a disgrace. "Despising the shame," do you know any phrase taken in its setting, more full of infinite majesty and splendour than that? "Despising the shame." Too often we perchance have endured the shame, and I do not say, despised the Cross, but forgotten it. He endured the Cross, despising the shame.

That was His consciousness; faith, things hoped for; the promise, faith in things unseen, God. He endured as seeing Him Who is invisible, and as the Rewarder of those who seek after Him; and in the strength of the former He endured the Cross and despised the shame.

So we reach the culminating word, "He sat down at the right hand of the throne of God." Try and write that sentence at the close of the sentences of any of those names. Take the finest and the outstanding, Abraham. . He sat down at the right hand of the throne of God? He could not do it. It would be impossible to do it. That can only be said of Jesus. Of no other could it be declared as the issue of personal triumph. In Him seated there faith has its last and unanswerable argument in a world such as this, and for pilgrims such as we are.

"Looking off." That is where I finish. "Looking off." God turn our eyes away from beholding man and men, the highest and the noblest and the best. If we look there we shall sooner or later be disappointed. If we look at ourselves we shall be worse than disappointed. "Looking off," see the witnesses. Yes, they are there, they are talking to us, they are speaking to us. See them, and then stop looking at them. "Looking off unto Jesus."

Well, if we do that, then what? I go back where I read at the beginning,

"We see not yet all things subjected to him."

That does not mean to Jesus. That means to man. The writer is quoting from the Psalm on the glory and dignity of man, that God had put all things under the foot of man. That is his place in the cosmic order. The writer says we do not see that yet. We do not see all things put under him.

Well, is not that disappointing? No. Why not? We see Jesus. "we behold Him." We behold the One Who is "crowned with glory and honour, that He should taste death for every man." That is the guarantee of the ultimate victory. That life of faith led Him all the way to Calvary; and in the mystery of that dying, faith is for evermore vindicated, His faith in God, in man, and in the future; and our faith in Him. "Looking off."

I hope our studies in these great illustrations have not been without value, but do not stay with them, do not linger with them. Hear their message, and quit the business of looking at them, "Looking off unto Jesus."

XVIII

Faith in the Present Times

SCRIPTURE LESSON - Mark xi. 12-14, 20-22; John xiv. 1, 7-11

"Have faith in God" - - - - - Mark xi. 22
"Ye believe in God, believe also in Me" - - John xiv. 1
"He that hath seen Me hath seen the Father" - John xiv. 9

W E have been considering the triumphs of faith as they are illustrated in the letter to the Hebrews, that section which begins in the tenth chapter and ends in the twelfth. The present meditation is intended to be a conclusion to the series, and is the outcome of a note which I received some time ago, in which the writer said:

"Would it be possible to reserve a little time at the end of your Faith Series to point out to us its adaptation to present times." I feel that the request is very pertinent and quite reasonable, and I want to reply to that request, which I think may represent the feeling of more than the one who wrote that little note.

I want to reply to it very briefly generally, and then to reply to it from the Biblical standpoint as revealed in the texts that I have chosen.

I confess that when I read that note I was a little perplexed. The stories we have considered are concerned with an abiding principle, and we considered that principle at the very outset of our meditations. It is the principle found in the prophecy of Habakkuk, and quoted in the New Testament, and it is found at the end of the tenth chapter of the letter to the Hebrews, introducing all we have been considering. In the Authorised reading the principle is declared in the words, "The just shall live by faith," or as we have it in the Revised, "My righteous one shall live by faith." But the principle is the same. It declares that the principle of life is faith. Please lay the emphasis on "live," "My righteous one shall *live* by faith." The principle of life, of whole life, of complete life, of real life, is faith.

Now all the stories have gathered around that abiding principle, and if they have illustrated anything—and we have seen that it is not a complete list, and the writer did not suggest it was—it is this, that circumstances are ever changing. Take the illustrations here,

121

beginning with Abel, with all that garden environment, coming on down through the ages until we get the varied portraiture with which in impetuous sentences the writer closes his illustrations, we are always conscious of different environment, different circumstances; but the principle never changes or varies, but has its application from the beginning and throughout all the stories and illustrations. The value of the stories is that they illustrate this principle, which never varies.

I want to say something in reply to that request, that I very much hope will not be misunderstood. However, I feel constrained to say it. It occurs to me that the request contained in that little note grows out of the contemplation of circumstances, and some failure to see God. I would say to that individual, believing that the request was perfectly honest, the secret of the difficulty is that you are looking at the times almost exclusively, and for the moment at least, if it be not true constantly, that your perplexity grew out of the fact that you were contemplating—I am quoting the phrase—"the present times," and failing to see God.

Now faith always is the result of the vision of God. Of course when I say vision, I do not mean any spectacular demonstration. That is what Philip wanted, "Show us the Father," some spectacular demonstrations. I mean the spiritual conviction of God. In that connection it is said of one, "He endured, as seeing Him Who is invisible." What a glorious paradox. What a glorious apparent contradiction. Can you see any thing that is invisible? Well, I can, and you can: the eyes of your understanding being enlightened, and your spiritual vision being clear, you can see God. "Blessed are the pure in heart, for they shall see God," said our adorable Redeemer, and He did not merely mean, if you are pure in heart you will see God by and by. You will see Him now, and everywhere. You can see Him in the flowers. You can see Him in all Nature. All that is very poor finally for the soul, but you can see Him. It is a trite commonplace, but it is magnificent and final, as Tennyson sang:

> "Flower in the crannied wall,
> I pluck you out of the crannies,
> I hold you here, root and all, in my hand,
> Little flower—but *if* I could understand
> What you are, root and all, and all in all,
> I should know what God and man is."

Yes, you can see Him everywhere, as you can see Him in all the movements of history; and the larger sweep you take in your outlook the more evident becomes the fact of God. Faith fastens upon that fact of God always. It is the vision of Him which is the inspiration of the faith which we have been considering. The faith that characterized all these men and women, these heroes and heroines, these witnesses and martyrs of the past, was the vision of God. If we lose that, if we allow the mists and clouds that are gathering about us to obscure that vision, then faith will fade.

How are we to apply this question of faith? I answer it at once, by seeing God. But let me turn from those generalities and ask you to look with me at these texts. All the words I read were words that fell from the lips of our Lord Himself, spoken in the last days of His earthly ministry. Probably there was about a week between the two occasions. The first was spoken to the disciples in view of the national failure. He was on His way to Jerusalem to excommunicate the Jewish nation from the high office it had held, and in which it had so appallingly failed. It was in that connection that He said to His disciples, "Have faith in God." The second and third of these words quoted and selected, were said to the same disciples a little later, in view of their future, and the responsibilities that would rest upon them as the result of the fact that they were to be His messengers, His witnesses in the world. To them He said, "You believe in God, believe also in Me . . . He that hath seen Me hath seen the Father." We take them for a moment in separation.

That first word, "Have faith in God." The occasion was the cursing and withering of the fig tree, and the disciples' astonishment at the swiftness of the carrying out of the sentence when on the next morning they saw the fig tree completely dead, withered. What a remarkable phrase that is, "Withered away from the roots." I am not concerned with any debates as to whether our Lord had any right to do that. To me to debate that is a supreme impertinence, whoever the theologian or expositor may be. It is always curious to me, that people who study botany do not hesitate to take a flower and pull the petals off, and pore into the mysteries and leave it dead, and yet they question His right to destroy a fig tree. Remember His right was inherent. The promise of figs should have been there, and there were none; and that was the whole point. The tree was dead in its roots while still maintaining an outward appearance of life. The action of our Lord there was intended to illustrate what He, from His kingly and august and Divine position was about to do with the Jewish nation. He was about to excommunicate it. In those last visits He had most definitely brought the whole nation before Him for trial in the most wonderful way. He told the rulers stories, or parables, asking their opinion, and they found the answer to every question He asked them. He appealed to them to find a judgment, and in every case they answered Him, and they were right. Their answers were right so far as the stories were concerned. Then they suddenly discovered He was talking to them: every story was an illustration of themselves and their failures. They had found a verdict against themselves. They had uttered a sentence against themselves. "He will miserably destroy those miserable men," is what they said. Then they found He was speaking of them, and they were angry. He then pronounced the sentence of excommunication. I never feel we can read it with sufficient solemnity until we grasp the profound significance of what He was saying, "The Kingdom of God shall be taken away from you, and shall be given to a nation bringing forth the fruits thereof." On His way He saw this fig tree. He knew that it was dead at the roots even then, and He pronounced His curse, and it came swiftly and suddenly: and the tree already dead at the roots before the the light of morning had withered. He was illustrating what He was doing, and giving the reason for it.

Now when His disciples drew attention to the dead tree, and were impressed with the suddenness of the death, it was then that He said to them, "Have faith in God."

Here I may run counter to a good deal of exposition. I rather like doing that sometimes when it is necessary. It is almost constantly said that He was telling them the secret of His power to curse the tree, that He was saying to them in effect, You see that tree withered in the night. The secret of the power is this, faith in God. I have faith in God. That is the general view. I submit to you that He meant nothing of the kind. He was not showing them the secret of the power, but declaring to them the reason of the nation's rejection, symbolized by the death of the tree. Why was the nation rejected? Because it had no roots. Its faith had failed. He said to those disciples, in view of that blasted fig tree before their eyes, with all that it symbolized in the national life of these people, Take care yourselves, have faith in God."

Do not let us forget that was the sin of the Hebrew people. The outward remained, the branches were spreading out of that tree, and it was clothed with leaves, but there was no fruit. Why not? It was already dead at the roots. From the roots it withered away. From the dead roots the whole tree shared in the blasting, and was withered away. That was the sin of the Hebrew nation. You

remember our Lord's description, "A faithless and perverse generation." That word "faithless" only occurs in the Gospels on the
lips of Jesus, and then only on two occasions. Matthew, Mark,
and Luke all refer to the fact that when He came down from the
mount of transfiguration and saw the boy in the valley, He said,
"O faithless and perverse generation." That is the word. The
other occasion, interestingly enough, was to Thomas, when after
the resurrection He said to him, "Be not faithless, but believing."
Now to His disciples as they looked on that withered tree, and He
directed their attention to all it meant, and they saw through the
symbolism of the cursing of the tree the blasting of a nation, He said,
"Have faith in God."

His call to the new nation, to His own people, what was it? See
God, have faith in Him, and view your "present times" and your
present circumstances, whatever they may be, from the standpoint
of that vision of God, and faith in Him.

I turn over from that great word to the Gospel according to
John, and here the occasion was different. He was talking to the
same men, but He was alone with them. Oh, the matchless wonder
of that section, chapters thirteen to sixteen. There is nothing of
this in any of the other Gospels. John has recorded for us those
intimate and final conversations of Jesus with that little group of
men who were going out presently. How wonderful they were.
How well He knew their weaknesses and failure. I began the
reading at the first verse of the fourteenth chapter, where we never
ought to begin, because we are interrupting the Lord. He was
saying something, but He did not begin there. Glance back to the
previous chapter. Peter is speaking—glorious, blundering and
splendid Peter. I am sure I am related to him because of the blunders
I have so often made. He said he would lay down his life for his
Lord, and he meant it. He never said a finer thing. But he did
not know himself, and he did not know the nature of the hurricane
that was so soon to sweep upon his Lord and upon himself. What
did Jesus say to him? Listen, and notice the change of number.
He began with a singular application, but at once introduces the
plural, which does not exclude the singular.

"Verily, verily, I say unto thee, The cock shall not crow, till
thou hast denied Me thrice. Let not *your* heart be troubled"—all of
them. Peter certainly, and all the rest. They were round about
Him, Peter with his honest and yet stupid boasting; and the Lord
said to him, Peter I know you better than you know yourself. I
know what is going to happen to you before the flush of morning

is upon the eastern sky. You, man of My choice, will have denied Me thrice. I can almost see the fear creeping over the faces of all of the disciples, especially Peter. But He has not done. "Let not your heart be troubled." Why not? "Ye believe in God, believe also in Me."

Then they went on. They were interrupting Him very honestly until Philip spoke, and to him He said, and to the rest also, "He that hath seen Me hath seen the Father." Alone with His own, facing the future, the hostile world massing its forces, conspiring against Him and against all His purposes, and the Cross lying right ahead. He had told them about it, but they had never grasped it. He is moving toward it, and knows directly He will reach it, but He is quite sure of the victory. Does He not say in the course of those last days, "Now is the judgment of this world." Judgment of this world? "Now shall the prince of this world be cast out. And I, if I be lifted up from the earth, will draw all men unto Myself." Yes, He knew the hostility. He knew the forces. He had plumbed the depths of the hurricane. He knew He was going to that to which they were going; but He said, "Do not let your hearts be troubled: you believe in God, believe also in Me."

Notice how He links their intellectual conviction of the past and recognises it. You believe in God. You believe, as this writer says, that God is. You believe that He is a Rewarder of those who diligently seek Him. Now I am calling you to link with that belief something else. I am calling you to accept the new interpretation of the God in Whom you believe that has come through Me: "believe also in Me." "He that hath seen Me hath seen the Father."

That is the whole thing. It is a stupendous claim, so simple and yet so absolutely sublime that one halts and worships in the presence of it, or else rejects it as sheer madness. We can take our choice. We cannot have it both ways: that He was mad, or an imposter, a fool; or else He was true to the men who had looked into those human eyes, and had seen God. That is what He said. "He that hath seen Me hath seen the Father."

What they saw of God in Him, and what it was intended that they should see of God in Him, was no contradiction of the past but a fulfilment of amazing significance.

Faith is due to the vision of God. Where shall I see God? In Him, and when we are puzzled by the present times, He is calling to us saying, "Let not your heart be troubled. You believe God, believe also in Me. . . . He that hath seen Me hath seen the Father."

If we want to see God so that our faith shall be complete, shall be vindicated, shall be firm and steadfast, see God in Him. That is what Christ was saying, and that is the whole truth of our Gospel. When Paul was writing to the Corinthians he wrote a tremendous sentence. I am content with the declaration, using Paul's words. "God was in Christ, reconciling the world unto Himself." The incarnation, God manifest; and God manifest for one purpose, that through the manifestation in all its completeness, He would reconcile the world to Himself.

Yes, the storms are gathering, the clouds are becoming more and more terrible. Hostility is roused throughout the world against our God and His Christ. "Let not your heart be troubled. Ye believe in God, believe also in Me." How shall we do it? "He that hath seen Me hath seen the Father." "God was in Christ," and that is not merely in life but in death; not merely the authority of all His teaching, but the actual personality, and the mystery of His atonement. "God was in Christ."

Well did His forerunner, looking upon Him as He stood upon the banks of the Jordan, say to those listening, "Behold the Lamb of God, which taketh away the sin of the world."

That is the application of faith to the present times. It is the same thing, the vision of God. But it is the vision of God granted to us now in Christ. The present times! We know so much about them, do we not? We read about them. The newspaper is really the mirror of the times. Look at the newspaper to-morrow morning, and see things there in the times mirrored. In every newspaper there is a mirror of the times. Do not forget that however fine, the mirror is concave, and very often it is convex, with the emphasis on the vex! Still there it is. "The times are out of joint." What is going to happen? You believe in God. Accept the interpretation of God that came to you through Christ. See that, and what will you see then? The focal point of the revelation is not found in the birth, is not found in the teaching, is not found in the wonderful miracles. Where is it found? On "the green hill, outside the city wall." If I want to see God I go to Calvary, and when I see God there, I find out that He is not indifferent, in spite of all the stupid things that stupid men are saying. I find that He is sharing in humanity's agony. He is bearing the results of its rebellion. I find He is bearing the sin of the world. "A body hast Thou prepared Me." He is bearing the sin of the world in that body. If I want to see God I see Him there, and I find that God is revealed there as sharing, bearing, suffering with suffering humanity in spite of all its sin. And I find that God is winning the victory that will open the gates for the return of man to Himself.

That is the application for the present times. Are we not in danger of forgetting it? Are we not in danger of going through the day and saying, "What is the news this morning? What do you think of the news this morning?" If you are tempted to ask that to-morrow morning, I will tell you something else. Pick up your New Testament for a few minutes, and go back to Corinthians. What is the news? "God was in Christ, reconciling the world unto Himself." That is God, and He is not indifferent, He is not distant. He is at hand, and through a mystery of pain that baffles our theologies and our philosophies, He is bearing the sin and making possible the way back, and that in spite of all the appearances of the present times.

You will remember those lines of Martin Luther written in dark and difficult days. I think they are very applicable to-day. Let me end with them:

> "We wait beneath the furnace blast
>   The pangs of transformation,
> Not painlessly doth God recast
>   And mould anew the nation
>
> "Where wrongs aspire;
>   Nor from the hand
>   That from the land
> Uproots the ancient evil.
>
> "Then let the selfish lips be dumb,
>   And hushed the breath of sighing,
> Before the joy of peace must come
>   The pains of purifying.
>
> "God give us grace
>   Each in his place
>   To bear his lot;
>   And, murmuring not,
>   Endure and wait the labour."

See God in Christ, and then look at the times.

Printed at the Press of the Publishers